THE GOSPEL OF FALLING DOWN

THE BEAUTY OF FAILURE, IN AN AGE OF SUCCESS

MARK TOWNSEND

Winchester, UK
Washington, USA)

First published by O Books, 2007
O Books is an imprint of John Hunt Publishing Ltd.,
The Bothy, Deershot Lodge, Park Lane, Ropley, Hants, SO24 0BE, UK
office1@o-books.net
www.o-books.net

USA and Canada
NBN
custserv@nbnbooks.com
Tel: 1 800 462 6420 Fax: 1 800 338 4550

Australia
Brumby Books
sales@brumbybooks.com
Tel: 61 3 9761 5535 Fax: 61 3 9761 7095

Singapore
STP
davidbuckland@tlp.com.sg
Tel: 65 6276 Fax: 65 6276 7119

South Africa
Alternative Books
altbook@global.co.za
Tel: 27 011 792 7730 Fax: 27 011 972 7787

Design: Stuart Davies
Cover design: Book Design, London

ISBN-13: 978 1 84694 009 5
ISBN-10: 1 84694 009 5

A CIP catalogue record for this book is available from the British Library.

Printed by Maple-Vail, USA

THE GOSPEL OF FALLING DOWN

THE BEAUTY OF FAILURE, IN AN AGE OF SUCCESS

MARK TOWNEND

Winchester, UK
Washington, USA

For my three angels, who continually teach me that
I am special as I am.

Jodie Jo - my darling fiancé
Aisha - my wonderful daughter
Jamie-Ash - my fantastic son

"I hope I do the same for you!"

CONTENTS

PREFACE

You are unique.

You are beautiful.

You are made in God's image.

There is no-one like you.

You are special.

You are once only.

You are never to be repeated.

You are incredible.

The above words are true for all people, yet many are unable to truly accept them. As a priest my hope is that, through this book, you will begin to discover your own true value as a human being made in the image of God. I want you to close the final page feeling somehow refreshed, liberated and able to *relax*, as if some huge weight has been removed. As a magician my hope is that you will have a renewed sense of magic and child-like wonder brought back into your life.

So, with this two-fold hope laid out before us let us step together through the metaphorical wardrobe and into a world of enchantment and discovery... *follow me!*

MARK TOWNSEND

ACKNOWLEDGEMENTS

Writing a book is not something I ever thought was possible for me. Yet, after many metaphorical 'bumps and bruises', and after bucket loads of encouragement from family and friends, a book has indeed materialised. I want to thank all those who have inspired, guided, supported and helped me along the way:
Richard Rohr, David Runcorn, James Alison, Eugene Burger, Mike Danata, Trevor Dennis, Patrick Duff, James Fahey, Caroline George, Jeff McBride, Robert Neale, Gerry Proctor, Rupert Sheldrake, Peter Spink, Stephen Verney, Frances Young, and all members of my family. Special thanks to Magician Dave Taylor (of Shop4Magic.co.uk) for the photography.
Also, huge thanks go to John Hunt for taking me (and my manuscript) seriously and making my dream of a book come true.

Bible quotations have been taken from:

FOREWORD

I first met Mark when he was training for ordination as a priest. We used to meet and talk about things that puzzled him. When he walked into the room I felt a sense of vitality. He was alive, and asking profound questions.

This little book is tackling one of the biggest and deepest questions which, unexpectedly, brings us to the foundation of the Christian faith. Mark has discovered this through his own experience of falling down, or failure.

His spiritual journey began with an intense 'conversion experience' within a small and loving Pentecostal church, but which has since then taken him through many traditions, and through experiences from the spiritual world outside the confines of the Church. He is also an accomplished magician and member of The Magic Circle. He sees these magical skills as something that can open people up to the state of wonder, mystery and awe which (he believes) the modern church, with all its changes for good, has sadly lost the ability to evoke.

This book is the result of him putting together his thoughts for a retreat which he was invited to conduct. The retreat had the same title, 'The Gospel of Falling Down,' and he was both surprised and delighted that it had a profound liberating affect on all who attended (me included). Here are a few comments from some of the participants:

'Fantastic! It has given me the chance to start to live the life or find the life of happiness I have a right to have. It was just incredible!'

'Wonderful, enchanting and uplifting. It has been an amazing experience for considering where I am at.'

'Concepts, new and exciting. Mind imploding!!'

'Not heavy but inspirational.'

'The realisation that failure can be creative would benefit many people. Keep saying these things Mark. They will unsettle people. The truth always does, but keep saying them.. I am so glad I heard them.. They are transforming me.'

I have written this as an endorsement of that final comment!

STEPHEN VERNEY.

INTRODUCTION

The Gospel of Falling Down – I imagine the title got you wondering, "How can falling down be good news? Surely the Gospel is about rising up!" And the sub-title, *The Beauty of Failure in an Age of Success* – "How can failure be beautiful? It doesn't look very pretty when I make a mess and have to face the humiliation of being laughed at or felt sorry for."

Rest assured, this book is not going to suggest that falling is *so good* for your soul that you should try to trip up more often. You are not going to be given a *how to* manual on the art of failure. The title comes, not from the warped mind of a masochistic writer who revels in humiliation and misery, but from the obvious and irrefutable fact that (from time to time, and whether we like it or not) we all make mistakes and fall down.

So, rather than introducing you to *'100 sure-fire methods of going arse over tip'* this book will suggest how we might view those falls (even redeem them) when they happen.

I have come to believe that such failures and flaws have a revelatory potential. They can offer us something priceless – a gift that we may never have discovered had we successfully kept ourselves perfect.

In the pages ahead I will be sharing many stories, personal anecdotes, and visual tricks. As a member of The Magic Circle I often use conjuring effects as object lessons to add visual drama and symbolism to my stories. For example I sometimes use a wonderful trick that dates back to the early 18th century called the

Fig 1) Fawkes performing the famous 'Egg Bag'

Egg Bag effect. Isaac Fawkes (c1675-1731), one of the most famous close-up conjurers of British history, held his audiences spellbound by the marvels he performed only inches from their eyes. He was known for his version of this baffling Egg Bag effect. From an apparently empty cloth bag, and to a delighted and ever more startled crowd of spectators, Fawkes would produce more and more eggs until they began to fall from the table and smash on the floor.

Fig 2) My Egg Bag

My version uses a small black cloth bag, and three eggs, one of which is gold coloured, a symbol of the inner treasure that is within all people. I wrote the following parable, both as a fitting story for the Egg Bag effect, and as a metaphor for the journey I hope this book will enable *you* to travel – a journey that may lead to unknown and even scary places, yet will bring you back to your own 'golden egg'.

THE EGG OF GOLD

They were an ordinary family, living ordinary lives, in an ordinary Russian village. Ordinary that is... until devastating famine struck!

The suffering was vast, and no one tasted the bitterness more than Nicholas' household.

Their only saving grace was their hen whose daily egg they relied upon... But she eventually died.

They were forced to sell everything – even Natasha's most treasured possession... a tiny painted wooden egg given to her by her grandma.

Their stomachs grew empty. Their world had been turned upside down, and inside out.

Nicholas heard a rumour of salvation – another hen – that laid golden eggs.

He took a chance and sought to find her. He tried hard but was too late. She lay lifeless, surrounded by the bodies of the desperate men who had fought over her.

Nicholas returned home in despair. His family were near death, their lives now cast into utter darkness. There was nothing left to sell. Nicholas glanced around his bare home, his eyes drifting from one place to another. Then he noticed the little bag that had once been used to store eggs. 'Oh how I wish you would provide us with one more', he sighed, but they all knew it was empty.

Yet an unexpected intuition came to the Russian peasant.

He cautiously placed his trembling hand into the dark interior of the bag and pulled out what his logical mind knew could not be there, yet what his heart knew would be there – a solid golden egg.

This book is about buried treasure, the kind of treasure we are told logically doesn't exist, but we feel must be there. Like a map, it will hopefully point you in the right direction to uncover it. This treasure is more valuable than any material thing you could possess. It is none other than the thing that you and I, and all people are searching for, even without knowing it. But this is not a book of answers. It is not another Book of Rules, or Set of Religious Certainties. There is nothing sacred about these words. Books cannot contain The Answer, neither can religions, priesthoods, philosophies, sacred texts nor holy men/women. These things are not answers but pointers to where The Answer *can* be found. The hidden treasure *is* The Answer, and it lies within.

CHAPTER ONE

LOOKING WITHOUT SEEING

'Once upon a time a group of friends went in search of a gold mine.

They searched for years but never succeeded in finding any gold. One day they were in a thick forest when one of them became sick and could walk no further, so the friends were forced to leave him behind and continued their search for gold. The sick man was very sad and was sitting under a tree thinking about his misfortune, when suddenly he saw a hole in which something appeared to be shining like gold.

He immediately started digging in the hole and, taking away the mud, found that he as sitting on a gold mine.

Humanity is walking on the gold mine of the kingdom of God but does not know it. Jesus came to reveal the eternal truth that the kingdom of God is everywhere, stop your searching and find that you are already in it. Blessed are you who have failed to find the kingdom of God because it is easy for you to realise that you are already in it.'

[1] **Brother John Martin Sahajananda.**

Many religious or spiritual books begin with the assumption that the goal of our longing is somewhere *out there*, and that our task is to constantly try to change ourselves into *this* or *that* before we have a hope of coming close to the goal. There is a kind of ideal that we feel we must aim for, and the closer we get to it, the nearer the goal comes. However if we believe we can ever achieve this goal by turning ourselves into the religious ideal then we have misunderstood the gospel of Christ, and the teaching of all the great spiritual traditions. It is not so much the attaining of that ideal but the *falling from it* that will, ironically, bring us closer to the *true* goal.

The title 'The Gospel of Falling Down' is a theme that dominates my life. It is a spiritual journey of three steps forward, two steps back. What I honestly hope that all my readers will come to value and understand, is that the two steps back (the falling) are as important as the three steps forward.

I am still considered to be a young man (thirty-nine years old to be precise), but even so it feels like I have been travelling this road for a long time.

The journey itself is one on which the further I travel, the more it seems I am not actually *moving* at all. Don't get me wrong, I am certainly growing and am gradually 'getting somewhere', but the 'somewhere' I am getting seems to be a place where I already am. Does this make sense? I am not talking about any physical destination that I am moving toward, nor am I talking about some new revelation of truth. I am talking about a process of *remembering what I had forgotten; of rediscovering what had long been covered up by mental clutter*.

I want to show you something. In a moment I am going to ask you to turn over to the next page and read the short passage in the centre of it. Then, as soon as you've read it once, go back and quickly count the times that the letter F is used in the passage. *But only do this once*. Just go through the passage counting the letter F. It should only take you about ten or fifteen seconds. Then *immediately* turn over to the next page.

Now without turning back to check, how many Fs did you count? Was it two, or three? Or could it have been more than that? Now turn over to the *next page* to see the correct answer.

You should have counted *SIX* letter Fs!

Is that a surprise? Go back to the page with the passage on and re-count…

Even when some people go back and re-count they still can't see the missing three Fs. Isn't that strange? They are there, as plain as daylight yet are almost invisible. We are for some reason temporarily blind to them. The trick works because it has been designed to fool the brain, which is surprisingly easy to do. While you are busy looking for the letter F, the brain is subconsciously trying to detect the sound of "f", as in *fire* or *face.* Because the sound of the letter f in 'of' is 'v', the brain causes you to overlook it.

There is another reason why this trick works. Not only does your brain look for the sounds that it expects to find in the passage, it also subconsciously looks for the mental images that words create. The brain can easily visualise the words *scientific, finished* and *files*, for example a scientific lab, a finished job, and an office file. But when trying to visualise 'of' it has nothing to create an image of, again making it seem invisible.

I find this fascinating, especially as a magician. Many illusions (large-scale or close-up) have been created by magicians who know very well that people *look without seeing.* Some of the cleverest stage illusions can fool the most scientific of minds, because such minds only see what they expect to see, and thus miss the trick that is going on right under their noses. I am not at liberty to explain the workings of any of these great works of magical genius, but I can give you an excellent example of this phenomenon that *does not* break the magician's code. When I was a teenager I remember being very impressed by a book about Kung Fu and other martial arts. It talked, in one place, about how to make yourself invisible and, believe it or not, when I tried the method it worked. It was all based on this notion of looking without seeing, and said that if you wish to become invisible, you must break the human form and try to blend in to the surroundings. I remember trying this technique with some friends. We were playing an elaborate form of hide and seek in a dark wooded area, and when my turn came I purposefully didn't hide. I simply stood close to a tree and tried to make my body, legs and arms non-human in shape – more like branches of a tree. It was uncomfortable but I was the only guy that could not be found, even though my friends came and stood only feet from where I was, looking straight at me. They saw nothing, for they were looking for a silhouette of a *human* shape, which made my 'broken human form' invisible.

The spiritual teachers of the East say that most of us spend our lives looking without seeing, missing what is right under our noses.

Spirituality is about seeing, waking up out of a deep sleep, remembering what was forgotten, cleansing the lenses. It is utterly astonishing what this new kind of seeing actually makes visible again, a part of ourselves that has been literally 'covered up' for years.

The journey that I was speaking about earlier is something like a gradual clearing away of the layers that the years of living in this world have added. The strange irony is that even when I discover a new 'revelatory thought or idea', it is *not new.* I already knew it, but would never have been reminded of it had I not been on this journey – this spiritual search. So the search that we often find ourselves upon *out there*, puts us in touch with the inner truth that we have chosen (or been caused) to forget *in here,* inside us. And it is my experience that the greatest times when the outer search brings us back in touch with the inner known truths are those times when we fail, fall and basically get our arses kicked by life. For me, I know that I am most able to catch a glimpse of the truth (the inner golden egg) after my outer shell, my outer religious (and perfectionist) self has taken a battering and become cracked.

One of the things that (we) religious people often do is try to change ourselves into what we think God and the Church want us to be like. I myself have been doing this for years, trying to be the perfect Christian. It's another part of my story, my quest to conform to some external religious blueprint.

No Christian denomination is truly free from this habit, though the 'ideal characteristics' of the *perfect Christian* differ depending on the type of church. I have been a member of a church where the perfect Christian would be a person who does not smoke, drink, swear or have any kind of romantic relationships with non-Christians. I have been a member of a church where you can do all those things as long as your politics are left wing and you never allow yourself to express any real certainty about matters of faith. I have also been a part of a church group where being respectable and well educated are the hallmarks of the perfect Christian.

There are also those who think that to be the perfect Christian means striving to become the most outwardly holy and pious person in the community. I have met many like this and have, from time to time, been drawn into this kind of behaviour myself. It is *false,* as are all the other pictures of Christian perfection. The fact is that if we try too hard to be the perfect Christian we will in fact be working *against* the current of God's transforming Grace rather than *with* it. Let me repeat that! If we try too hard to be the perfect Christian we will in fact be working *against* the current of God's transforming Grace rather than *with* it.

You see, if we think we can turn ourselves into the perfect Christian, we have missed the point of the entire Gospel, and will be making the Christ within us harder to see, not easier. We will be adding more layers and more clutter that one day will simply have to be removed (usually by falling down).

If this sounds too much like heresy (and it might) all I ask is that you give it a chance. If you come to the conclusion that it is utterly wrong, then simply forget what you've read and file the book in such a place as to stop it from doing any more harm. But just allow me to share with you a remarkable quotation from a spiritual writer with a universally agreed authority (within the Church).

The following passage could I think easily be entitled 'On the Gospel of Falling Down':

> *"And then he [God] allows some of us to fall more severely and more distressingly than before – at least that is how we see it. And then it seems to us, who are not always wise, that all we set our hands to is lost. But it is not so. We need to fall, and we need to see that we have done so. For if we never fell we should not know how weak and pitiable we are in ourselves. Nor should we know the wonderful love of our maker.*
>
> *In heaven we shall see truly and everlastingly that we have grievously sinned in this life, notwithstanding we shall see that this in no way diminished his love, nor made us less precious in his sight.*
>
> *The testing experience of falling will lead us to a deep and*

wonderful knowledge of the constancy of God's love, which neither can nor will be broken because of sin. To understand this is of great profit."

[2] **Julian of Norwich.**

And, for those who might be a little unimpressed with my quoting from a medieval saint/mystic let me perhaps remind you of some passages from the very foundational document of the church, the New Testament. I have chosen one from each of the four gospels and one from Paul's letters. They could be grouped together and given the title: 'New Testament sayings on finding the way through doing it wrong'.

'While Jesus was having dinner at Levi's house, many tax collectors and 'sinners' were eating with him and his disciples, for there were many who followed him. When the teachers of the law who were Pharisees saw him eating with the 'sinners' and tax collectors, they asked his disciples: "Why does he eat with tax collectors and 'sinners'?"

On hearing this, Jesus said to them, "It is not the healthy who need a doctor, but the sick. I have come not to call the righteous, but sinners."'

Mark 2:15-17 (NIV)

[Jesus said] "There was a man who had two sons. He went to the first and said, 'Son, go and work today in the vineyard.'

'I will not,' he answered, but later changed his mind and went.

Then the father went to the other son and said the same thing. He answered, 'I will sir,' but did not go. Which of the two did what his father wanted? 'The first,' they answered."

Jesus said to them, "I tell you the truth, the tax collectors and the prostitutes are entering the kingdom of God ahead of you. For John came to you to show you the way of righteousness, and you did not believe him, but the tax collectors and the prostitutes did. And even after you saw this, you did not repent and believe him."

MATTHEW 21:28-32 (NIV)

Now the tax collectors and 'sinners' were all gathering round to hear him. But the Pharisees and the teachers of the law muttered, "This man welcomes sinners, and eats with them."

Then Jesus told them this parable: "Suppose one of you has a hundred sheep and loses one of them. Does he not leave the ninety-nine in the open country and go after the lost sheep until he finds it? And when he finds it, he joyfully puts it on his shoulders and goes home. Then he calls his friends and neighbours together and says, 'Rejoice with me; I have found my lost sheep.' I tell you that in the same way there will be more rejoicing in heaven over one sinner who repents than over ninety-nine persons who do not need to repent."

LUKE 15:1-7 (NIV)

The teachers of the law and the Pharisees brought in a woman caught in adultery. They made her stand before the group and said to Jesus, "Teacher, this woman was caught in the act of adultery. In the Law Moses commanded us to stone such women. Now what do you say?" They were using this question as a trap in order to have as a basis for accusing him.

But Jesus bent down and started to write on the ground with his finger. When they kept on questioning him, he straightened up and said to them, “If any one of you is without sin, let him be the first to throw a stone at her.” Again he stooped down and wrote on the ground.

John 8:1-8 (NIV)

[Paul writes] To keep me from becoming conceited because of these surpassingly great revelations, there was given me a thorn in the flesh, a messenger of Satan, to torment me. Three times I pleaded with the Lord to take it away from me. But he said to me “My grace is sufficient for you for my power is made perfect in weakness.”

Therefore I will boast all the more gladly about my weaknesses, so that Christ’s power may rest on me. That is why, for Christ’s sake, I delight in weaknesses, in insults, in hardships, in persecutions, in difficulties. For when I am weak, then I am strong.

2Corinthians 12:7-10 (NIV)

CHAPTER TWO

'Only those who have reached the limit of themselves, with nothing to offer in their own defence, fall into the abyss of love. In fact only sinners understand the gospel. It is not available to anyone else.'

[3] **David Runcorn**

THE BROKEN THREAD

Fig 3) The Incredible Eugene Burger

I've been enchanted by magic and illusion for as long as I can remember. It has had a profound ability to keep alive the experience of mystery and wonder, which has been so important for me. As I have progressed in my own magical skills and knowledge, I have unashamedly used it to awaken others to that same experience of enchantment. Of course I do not claim any special powers. I simply allow the power of the magical experience itself to carry people into the world of childlike wonder and awe.

There is another reason why magic is so powerful. Not only does it evoke wonder, it also taps into some of the deepest longings and hopes of humankind. When I see a good stage illusionist I often feel like I'm a participant in a religious ritual. The visual images can reach places within our psyches that are usually assumed to be the domain of religion alone. Take for example the so-called cut and restored effects. Most magic performances, of whatever style, will include one or two tricks where something (or someone) is apparently broken or destroyed, and yet restored again. Perhaps it is a rope, or a spectator's shiny new watch, or a bank note, or even a volunteer from the audience.

When we watch something being broken, torn up or smashed, it resonates deep inside because we have all (regretfully) experienced the destructive side of life. You don't have to spend many years in this world to learn that some things will break if you drop them. The experience of brokenness is simply a fact of life for us all, and I'm not just talking about physical breaking. Many of us have also had more than a taste of emotional brokenness too. Consider some of the following sayings and ask yourself whether you've ever used any of them in reference to your own life: broken promise, broken heart, damaged relationship, bruised ego, shattered dream…

The first part of the cut and restored trick, therefore, emotionally pulls us into the experience by ruthlessly exposing us to a display of destruction. It is entertainment, and we are excited, but we are easy prey because we have that inner emotional hook – the fact that we know what *to break something* means. We *know* that life is fragile.

But the trick does not stop there. It does not leave us with that uncomfortable feeling of witnessing something being destroyed. If it did it might be symbolic, but it would not be magic. No, the magic comes when the magician says or does something to make the broken item whole again. One cannot over state how powerful this can be, for just as we all know what it means to witness something (even ourselves) being broken, we also know what it means to hope or dream for healing and restoration.

I use a very well known cut and restored trick as a visual aid for a story I wrote which I called The Broken Thread. The trick has had a long pedigree in magic, and, like the Egg Bag, goes back many centuries. It is usually known as the Gypsy Thread, and involves a long piece of yarn that is unwound, cut in various places, and then 'magically restored'. I have borrowed a method made famous by the enchanting Chicago-based magician Eugene Burger, under whom I recently had the privilege of being taught.

To a powerful Hindu story of creation, destruction and re-creation, Eugene will dramatically unwind the thread over a candle, and use the flame to symbolically burn it into five or six pieces. Finally he will wind up all but one of the pieces into a ball, press the ball onto the remaining piece of thread and leave it there, adding silence for effect. Then at the perfect moment he will gaze into your eyes, grab the two ends of the single strand (with the ball pressed on to it) and majestically stretch it out into one long restored thread.

The 'cut and restored' aspect of the Gypsy Thread trick illustrates well the story's theme, which is about the inner turmoil and brokenness of a rather guilt-ridden soul who, because of his own sense of failure, feels more and more cut off from God. The character feels as though he is hanging on by a thread, and yet even that thread eventually snaps. The restoration comes, not because God suddenly decides to forgive, but because the guy suddenly discovers that God was not who he thought He was, and the thread was *never* broken at all. I wrote the story as a participant on a beautiful retreat led by the master storyteller, Trevor Dennis.

The following images show the various stages of the effect:

Fig 4) Thread is unwound and stretched out over flame

Fig 5) Thread is broken in various places

Fig 6) All but one of the pieces are wound up into a ball

Fig 7) Ball is pressed onto the remaining strand

Fig 8) Thread is stretched out again, now fully restored

THE BROKEN THREAD

The Church was dark – darker than I had ever seen it, save for the solitary candle left as a flickering symbol of the last pilgrim's prayer. This offering of wick and wax melted away in front of the austere icon of Christ the King, and, before that terrifying portrayal of God, I too began to melt. Melt, not as a lover's heart melts in the arms of her beloved, but more as a puppy's will melts in submission before his cruel and punishing new master's raised right arm. Yet I found strength to speak.

'My God', I cried, 'why do you have to look at me like that? You frighten the hell out of me. Why do you have to glare down with such severity, looking, so it seems, in aristocratic disgust at the pathetic creature beneath your feet? Why do I continually feel unworthy and unlovable – a mere worm to be trodden on, a fly to be squashed? My God you know I've tried –- tried so damn hard to please you. I've bust my back trying to achieve all those requirements set out by your 'representatives'. Yet I still feel rotten to the core.

I feel like I'm hanging on by a thread. I'm clinging to a sky-high tightrope stretched out across a treacherous chasm. I'm trying to inch my way across to salvation, but a hurricane wind's bent on shaking me off into the flaming pit below. Maybe I should just let go? Maybe you want me to. Maybe the red-hot fire – the hell hot fire – is your way of purging me of my sins. Yet, if I do drop, I fear I'll be purged out of existence.

My God, any moment this rope between us is going to break. I've let you down so many times – and each time I've felt some of the fibres give way.

Here it comes – your judgement!

Lack of faith – SNAP!

Poor church attendance –SNAP!

Looking at that woman – SNAP!

Losing it with my kids – SNAP!

My God, the thread between us is in tatters.'

I looked down, too numb to cry, yet what I saw made me tremble. There, on the floor, beneath my feet, glistening with candlelight ripples, was a pool of water, no! a pool of tears. I slowly followed their path – up and up – to the very face of Christ – the very eyes of God. I stood, motionless, gazing into love's stare, my eyes now wet as his. And, after what seemed like an eternity, he spoke:

'My child! My precious, precious child. How it crucifies me to see – to feel – your pain. Your failure has not been your faith or your actions. No! Your only mistake has been to believe the words of misguided men, men who've poisoned my good news and turned it sour, men who've put price tags on my free gift of Grace, unhappy men who've projected their own worst nightmares, their own darkest shadows, onto me, and have thus unintentionally created a god in their own image.

My child, I was never far from you, nor will I ever be. Even if you do ever cease to believe in me, I will never cease to believe in you. I don't require sacrifices or ego-effort. I don't expect sinless perfection. My kingdom is not a meritocracy, my Grace is free, and my love is unconditional. And, be sure of this, the thread that holds us together – that binds us together – will never, ever be broken.'

In a way that story says everything that I want to say, for it sums up what I most hold to be true about the GOD of unconditional love. It also portrays the Church's failure to present the Gospel, leaving the poor guilt-ridden soul little chance of finding the Gospel of Grace.

But I know that I can't just offer that story and say, 'There you go, run along now and live within God's unconditional love'. Why? Because experience has taught me that many people (particularly Christians) do not accept that God's love *is* unconditional. If I am honest, a part of me doesn't even accept it. I often say from the pulpit that *I* am the person who most needs to hear and truly understand this. *I KNOW* the truth, but to allow it to penetrate every cell of my being is another matter entirely.

Religious faith can be a double-edged sword. It can be Good News that cuts through our chains and liberates us into a new sense of self worth as being made in the image of God. But it can also come across as Bad News, for there are those who see it only as a rule against which to measure our every thought, word and action, with the consequence of divine disapproval and punishment should we not measure up. The next chapter is going to plunge you into the story of my own *fall* into this sense of extreme divine disapproval, but it will not leave you there. There *is* another side to the picture, and yes *it is* Good News.

AN EXERCISE:

At this point I'd like to introduce you to a little (optional) exercise. It's a two-part exercise, the second half of which will come at a later stage in the book.

Find a large sheet of paper and some crayons or coloured pens. Don't worry if you find drawing difficult, this is not an art lesson. I'd like you to try to draw a picture of God. Don't think too much about it. Just close your eyes for a while, imagine what you think God might be like, and draw what you see. If you find this impossible, try to imagine something that reminds you of God, or something that symbolises God. A tree perhaps, or a rainbow. Draw what you see.

When you have finished do not try to analyse your drawing but keep it somewhere safe so that at the end of the book it can be looked at again.

CHAPTER THREE

MY STORY OF FALLING DOWN

"When I started working with young people in the early 70s I spent a lot of time trying to convince teenagers that they were good. They all seemed endlessly, bottomlessly to hate themselves. Later... ...I found it wasn't just teenagers but adults, too. They endlessly hate themselves, doubt themselves and have to spend most of their energy to feel good about themselves."

[4] **Richard Rohr.**

One of the most useful tools for the spiritual life is keeping a journal. I have done so, on and off, for about twenty years and would recommend the practise to anyone. It doesn't have to be a heavy task. My journal is simply an A4 ring binder containing a pad of paper. Over the years I have tried to jot down any thoughts or experiences that were spiritually interesting or enlightening. The fact that it is a ring binder means that, even when I'm away on holiday or far from home, I can still get hold of some paper to write on which can be clipped into my binder on my return. I often write poems or stories, or even prayers to God, all of which go into my journal.

Recently I decided to re-read the whole journal, but I had no idea of how much the contents were going to surprise me. As I began reading each entry I started to detect a clear pattern in my experiences.

This is what I wrote on 2 August 1990. As I remember, I had been trying to give up smoking again, and had had a few too many drinks the night before which led to me re-start the roll ups. At that point in my life I had not long left a friendly little Pentecostal Church to become an Anglican. The 'culture' of the church I had left was rather prohibitionist. No one was *told* what or what not to do but we all knew certain things were bad or even of the devil. Among these things were clearly smoking, drinking, pubs and clubs.

I have not corrected or tidied up the following quotation in any way, and it may well seem 'very young'. *I was!*

A LETTER OF CONFESSION

"My Father, Lord and Saviour of Mankind. God who gave up everything in order to create a way possible for the redemption of mankind, have mercy on me. I have woken up today plagued by guilt and self-hatred. I can't understand how a man like me, who used to have such self-control and will power, can so easily fall back into my old way of living. Have I lost the fear of God? I think not. Rather, I feel I have sub-consciously or unconsciously watered down the 'Way of the Cross' to suit my own condition.

Father, I again use the phrase 'I repent', but before I do please help me to mean it. I wish to be able to put an end to my desire for alcohol, which leads to tobacco. I wish to put a stop to laziness and half-hearted worship. Help me to love you and your way much more than my bookshelf. Help me to fear you and be afraid of your wrath so I might learn to be a better example of your saving grace.

I repent Lord. I turn again from my disgraceful ways. Help me I pray, and have mercy on me, a sinner. In the name of Jesus. AMEN."

This is an example of 'one-half' of the 'pattern' that I was beginning to detect in my re-reading of the journal. It was an obsessive feeling of unworthiness, self-hatred and perfectionism. Along with this was also a regular *need* to go through little written rituals of repentance.

I remember, even before I began writing a journal, I used to write pledges or promises to God in books and other places saying 'this time I will be good' etc…

The things I didn't like about myself were not that bad, but they pointed to an underlying feeling that *in myself I was simply not good enough.* For some reason I had ended up becoming a young man who felt really shit about himself. I desperately wanted to be someone else, and had an obsession with trying to change. At one point I even tried to join the Royal Marines thinking this would gain me approval, acceptance and a better sense of being someone. So I put myself through three days of mental and physical hell only to be turned down at the end because I "didn't show enough aggression". Surprise, surprise!

Now is not the place to go into psychological theories about current lack of youth self-esteem (or self-value). Plenty of books have been written on it. It is enough to say that millions of young people in the West are sadly growing up feeling inadequate, unworthy, and not good enough.

But I was a *Christian* when I was writing these things! Surely a Christian shouldn't be tormented by such self-hatred! Well, I'm afraid I was doing what many Christians and even some whole denominations do. I was projecting my own false images onto God. They were images I had learned from this first part of my life; hostile images where value, approval and love are not freely given but earned, and are utterly conditional.

I was mentally creating a *God* in the image and likeness *of humans*. And as I continued to write entries into my journal this 'God' showed up time and time again. Sometimes it was explicit, but often, especially in the more recent entries, it has been more hidden. Over the last few years my preaching and teaching has almost entirely been about Grace, forgiveness, and unconditional love, *yet* there are still pages and pages of journal notes that express guilt, unworthiness and perfectionism.

When I look back at the last decade of my life I can see how dominant this self-critical and unworthy side to my character has been. There have been points where the feeling of total inadequacy has become so intense that I have come close to a complete breakdown. In fact in the summer of 2000 I was actually signed off work for six weeks, sent to a counsellor and put on a course of anti-depressants. Many things led to that 'fall' but the stress I allowed to build up by *trying to achieve* was one of the overriding factors.

It's hard enough for someone in a regular job to admit to a so-called breakdown, but for a *clergyman?* Talk about humbling experiences!

The only thing that was more humbling than that was having to tell my congregation that my wife and I were separating. That came a year or so after the 'breakdown'. Again there's no need to go into the whys and ifs of that saga. It's enough to say that, like any separation (especially where children are involved) it was humiliating, painful, and a bloody big ‘fall’.

However, *and this is what really knocked me over,* as I looked again at my journal, I started to detect another *different* voice within my writings.

CHAPTER FOUR

THE 'TWO VOICES'

(Fig 9) **Anonymous**

If you have never come across the above picture you are in for a treat, for it is a lovely visual trick. What you need to do is fix your full attention on the four dots near the centre of picture for 30 seconds. As soon as you have done so tilt your head backwards and look at the ceiling above (make sure it is a plain light ceiling). You will gradually begin to see a circle of light. Keep looking at the circle. Don't try to force anything, just wait for the magic to happen…

I fell in love with that visual trick from the first moment I saw it. Not only did it surprise me by turning a muddle of black splodges and dots into a lovely image of Jesus, it also reminded me that beneath the veneer of my own shallow public persona is a wiser hidden self, *another voice,* who just occasionally I become aware of.

I first became aware of this other voice when I re-read my journal, but since then I have been aware of it in many other places. For example I can sometimes detect it within my sermons, letters to the local newspaper, articles in the parish magazine, stories, poems, and magic tricks that involve a storyline.

I don't want to give the impression that I have a split personality. I am not talking about 'voices' in that sense. I am talking about what I now call the little-me and the Divine-Me, the two distinct voices within us all. The little-me corresponds to the voice I was speaking of in the previous chapter, whereas the Divine-Me is something else completely.

At this point it might help if we look briefly into the world of eastern meditation. Many spiritual teachers talk of meditation as the practise of awareness. When you sit in a meditative state, you gradually become alert to all that is happening now and are able to sense and feel things that are often covered up by the ordinary experiences of life. You also become aware of particular thoughts entering and leaving the mind (some good, some not so good). Spiritual teachers often advise us to just observe these thoughts, and let them go; not to judge them, just to recognise them and be aware of them passing through the mind.

Now, stop there for a moment! The fact that in meditation 'you can observe your own thoughts' means that there is a YOU who is watching *you.* The *you* that is the constant flow of thoughts ('What's on TV?,' 'Oh God I wish I could sit still,' 'I wonder how my sermon was received this morning?') is now *being observed* by *YOU*. The little you of all those thoughts is now being observed or watched by something *much bigger*. This observer (this *something much bigger*) is what I call the Divine-Me.

What I have come to see is that, at various points in my life, especially when certain trauma has forced me to 'let it all out' with a pen and paper, I sometimes get in touch with a deeper part of my consciousness – a quieter, wiser Self – the Divine-Me.

So, these 'two voices' that I detected in my journal, sermons and so on are what I now choose to refer to as the little-me and the Divine-Me. And I want to say forcefully that we all have this little-me, *and we all have this Divine-Me.*

The little-me is called by some writers the ego or the false self. I feel that the term little-me is less negative than either of those terms.

The little-me is egocentric; concerned with self-preservation, and is rather inward looking. It has a habit of being judgemental, both to self and to others. It is critical, insecure, needy, defensive and proud. The little-me is only ever secure in achievement and is therefore highly fragile and easily offended. The little-me wants to control and manage, and cannot easily let go.

On the other hand the Divine-Me is God-centred (which also means self-less), unconcerned with self-preservation, outward looking, forgiving, fair, content. The Divine-Me is secure without the need of achieving; secure because of being made in the image and likeness of God. The Divine-Me has the natural ability to 'Let Go and Let God'. The Divine-Me is un-offendable.

Of course my story 'The Broken Thread' was a good example of my little-me talking to, and being replied to, by my Divine-Me.

Here is a more recent example. As you read it you will notice that I was very much in my little-me state. I was tired and desperately trying to think of something to say for Ash Wednesday, yet nothing was coming. It is written as a dialogue between me and God. I want you to read it as a dialogue between the little-me and the Divine-Me.

A PRE-ASH WEDNESDAY PRAYER DIALOGUE

"Oh well, here I am Lord, sitting down at the end of a particularly busy and stressful day. You know how demanding this week has been. You know what a huge backlog of work I've stupidly allowed to build up. And you know what extra stuff – really important stuff – has come in today. I don't even know where to begin. And now I am pathetically tired.

My God, what do I do? And what am I going to say to the people next Wednesday as we enter Lent? Come on, help me. Give me something to say. Give me a way through some of this stress and overload. I'm falling asleep at this damn computer, and I am starting to panic."

"Mark, go to bed. You can't hear what I want to tell you when you are trying so hard. Let go of trying for tonight. Get an early night and sleep. Then you will be more rested and better able to not get in the way of the inner voice. But as you go to sleep be aware of the greater sleep. 'Remember that you are dust and to dust you shall return' Remember that you are just a passing visitor to this

planet. A hundred years from now and your physical self will just be a distant memory. The things that you worry about and lose sleep over will also be long gone."

"Look God, I don't want to go to bed now. I am still panicking. I am still worried that I won't get everything done."

"Mark, you are a stubborn fool! Now give up, surrender, and go to bed. Let go… trust me."

(LONG PAUSE)

"OK. You were right. I slept like a baby. I do feel more refreshed and peaceful. But still there is so much to do."

"Do, Mark! Yes, there are always things to do, but most of them are not as urgent as you imagine. Rather than do, you ought to be learning how to be. Remember that you are dust and to dust you shall return. And when you do return to dust you will have not completed or achieved all that you wanted to. That's the fact. There will always be things in your 'in tray' Mark. You will never come to the bottom of the pile. Peace will finally come to you not by eliminating these tasks or working all night to clear your desk. No, peace will only come when you learn to view them from a different perspective.

When you remember that 'you are dust' the things that so pressurise you lose some of their power over your happiness. And the more important things become a higher priority in your mind. You humans, Mark, are hoarders, gatherers, collectors, and not

only of material things. You collect problems, ambitions, desires, goals, apparent responsibilities. You will find me not by collecting even spiritual ambitions, but by precisely the opposite – by giving up, by letting go, by surrendering, by being, by remembering and acting on the truth that you are dust and to dust you shall return."

"But does that mean I am just dust, Lord? Does that mean I have no real value in myself? Am I worth so little?"

"Oh Mark, how easy it is for you to misunderstand and hear what you want to hear. No of course you are not just worthless dust. In fact you are worth so much – indeed you are priceless, as is every other person on this planet. The problem is that so few of you believe it! So then your egos kick in and you try to become what you think will make you valuable. You fail to see your interior riches when you chase after external achievements and place all value in them. Are you really any less 'Mark' when you fail at that project or don't make the grade at that exam? No, of course not, and the irony is that you are more likely to catch a glimpse of your inner beauty when you DO fail at achieving your external goals. You may well get low and enter a symbolic desert for a while, but the desert is the place where you will find your divine self. You see, in such places there is no way you can rely on your achievements or goals; all you have is what you are. Naked, empty, powerless – and staying with that human emptiness WILL bring you in contact with your true inner treasure.

To enter the desert and to remember that you are dust, Mark, helps you to see reality as it really is – that most of your concerns

are about things that simply don't matter. Most of your fears are about clinging onto an illusion. Your ego-self Mark, your outer shell, the little Mark who demands praise, who hates criticism, who feels threatened, who is a perfectionist, who gets defensive and offended, who wants to be the best priest and so on… that is the dust that is here today and tomorrow has no reality. If you can truly come to see that then you will be liberated, and will wake up into a new state of being."

"Oh God, so much of what I am about comes from the hopes, dreams, ambitions, and desires of what you call the ego. And you are right; it is when I don't gain a goal, or when I desire praise but only get criticism, or when I struggle to be perfect, that I am most unhappy."

"You are not alone Mark; nearly every other person on this planet is in the same place. And you religious ones make it worse by suggesting that you can come to know me by following these rules or that practice or by getting better at being spiritual. That all comes from the false self – the ego. The fact is, I am already as present as I ever could be in the heart of all. And any attempts to find me 'out there' only hinder the discovery that I am closer than breath itself. Mark, if you want something to learn this LENT, use it as a time to enter the desert within; and lead the others there too. Find me – your ever-present treasure – within your own inner wilderness."

"But Lord, when your son faced the desert he resisted many temptations. He seemed to achieve a high level of spirituality

during that time. How do we try to mirror that?"

"Stop it Mark! You speak from the ego again. YOU do not need to TRY. You do not need to attain, especially what you call a high level of spirituality. There is no such thing as levels of spirituality. There is only being. By being and by knowing that the ego's goals and desires are illusions, Jesus in his desert resisted them. He knew that he already had everything. He could not be added to by any pathetic gift of the ego. The three temptations were about facing what we all face: power, possessions and position. The ego promised him worldly power and glory – and he was tempted – who wouldn't have been. But look carefully; these ego-gifts were not what many of you associate with sin – no, they were what most of you see as respectable, good things. And they can be. But what Jesus did was to pave the way for all of us, and give us an eternal sign that these things – wealth, power, name, respectability, image, reputation, honour and so on, can never bring true happiness in themselves. They should never be placed on a pedestal, as if life is about working up to some great goal or achievement. Jesus knew he already had everything that he needed, to be who he truly was.

When we learn to let go of relying on external rewards and labels we will gradually become more real, and consequently more secure."

"OK God, I will start to try and deny myself some of the luxuries I enjoy. I know this Lent I'll give up more – I'll give up booze, chocolate, Indian meals and coffee."

"You are truly amazing Mark! How can you miss the point time and time again? I am not talking about giving up trivial pleasures for LENT. What good will six weeks of abstinence do for you apart from feed your spiritual ego and give you a pharisaic sense of superiority over those who have less will power? Mark, the desert is the place where you discover and face who you truly are, with all your inner demons and darkness, not try to avoid who you are by denial. You are falling into the trap that the majority of Christian people fall into. You are creating a division – a separation between body and soul. You Christians have divided the universe into a state of separation. Unbeliever from believer, Catholic from Protestant, Conservative from Liberal – MARK THERE IS NO SEPARATION IN ME. THERE IS ONLY UNION.

So, rather than punish your body, try to love it. Love who you are, spend time in prayerful awareness and learn who you really are, and when you discover your own inner emptiness and weakness, don't rush out to fill it with another ambition, or activity, or addiction – go further into it and discover the HIGHER POWER, who is your ever present strength.

I've said enough Mark, enough to blow your mind, and confuse all the others. Be patient with yourself, and enter the desert knowing you are not alone. You will get lonely, but by staying with it and not avoiding it with substitute fixes, you WILL DISCOVER THE REALITY OF THE PRICELESS JEWEL THAT EXISTS RIGHT NOW WITHIN."

EXERCISE:

During my retreat I led a session with the subtitle 'Epistles to

Ourselves' where I gave the participants an exercise to do overnight and asked them to share the experiences the next morning. The effects were profound.

The first part of the exercise involved finding a quiet moment and writing a letter to God, expressing any thoughts, feelings or questions that came to mind. Then, for the second part, I suggested that the participants try to write a reply to their own letter as if from God.

I must emphasise the words 'as if from' here. I am **not** *claiming that this exercise puts us in touch with God himself, and the replies to the letters are* **not** *modern day Biblical epistles. However, the experience of prayerfully imaging what God might want to say to you can potentially open yourself up to the deeper voice of the Divine-Me. Of course this is a manufactured exercise, whereas the examples I gave from my own spiritual journal were natural and happened without me trying to get in touch with a deeper self. Even so, the participants on the retreat were utterly surprised by what they themselves had written when they shared their letters to the group.*

You will find an example of one of these letters in Appendix 2, at the back of the book.

CHAPTER FIVE

OBSESSED WITH SUCCESS

We are so used to describing Jesus' cross and resurrection as a victory that we easily forget that what that victory looked like was a failure. So great is the power behind Jesus' teaching and self-giving that he was able to fail, thus showing once and for all that 'having to win', the grasping on to meaning, success, reputation, life and so on is of no consequence at all.

[5] **James Alison.**

'Every religion creates her own ego'

[6] **Brother John Martin Sahajananda.**

The Church, being a human institution, has its own corporate ego, or collective 'little-me'. And just as the little-me is sometimes such an obvious and controlling characteristic of human individual, so the same is true for the Church. We ought to forgive the Church for this, though it is understandable that many cannot. The immense hurt that has been caused by the defensive and sometimes very punishing little-me of the Church cannot be over exaggerated. I'm certain the same is true for every religion.

One of the signs of the Church's little-me is of course its divided state and its denominationalism. The glorious diversity that denominations bring is a blessing, but fighting over who is right and who is wrong, or who is saved and who is damned is destructive, and entirely egocentric. Again, remember, each denomination has its own little-me.

A Church that is driven by the little-me will have a very difficult time in proclaiming the Gospel of Unconditional Love, and I don't believe any particular denomination has been any better than any other at presenting the Gospel. Every sect and tradition within the Church has its own passion and 'slice of the truth', but each one has also ended up with its own flaws in presenting that truth.

Jesus once told a parable about treasure hidden in a field, and the person who knows it's there goes out and sells all he has to purchase not just the treasure, *but the whole field,* which presumably includes all the not so treasure-like bits too (Matthew 13:44).

I happen to love the particular 'field' I live in, which is the Church of England. I love it, though it sometimes drives me crazy.

So let's not assume that any one denomination has a monopoly on the truth.

But what *is* the truth of the Gospel, the truth that sets us free? What is the Good News that we want to taste and share and pour out for the whole world to see?

Well, first let me suggest what it is not. The Gospel is not about *success*. Did you hear me? I said the Gospel is not about success! To make the Gospel into a means of being successful is to seriously miss the point. We live in a success-dominated world, and much of the (especially Western) Church has become a success-dominated religion.

What is the central symbolic image for the Christian faith? It's a cross of wood, with a figure of a man nailed to it – a naked, bleeding man. A man so wounded, so humiliated, so crushed that one can barely imagine what this scene was actually like in reality. But try if you can to picture the scene… Now add to the picture the fact that this man was somehow also God! Success?

And what does this bleeding, crucified God promise us?
Worldly protection – *NO!*
Wealth – *NO!*
Respectability – *NO!*
Privilege – *NO!*
Physical, material or emotional security – *NO!*
Marriages that never fail – *NO!*
Employment that lasts – *NO!*
Membership of the only true religion – *NO, NO, NO!*

SO WHAT DOES HE PROMISE US?

Unconditional Love and acceptance as *we are.* God promises us a spiritual home and welcomes us in without having to do anything other than step through the door. We are valued and loved and held without first having to change and seek approval. We are God's sons and daughters, and do not have to feel like outsiders, as if we do not belong. And this is LIFE! Yes, new life. Or should I say a NEW experience of life, for it is no longer about the fragile quest of attaining and maintaining sinless perfection, but receiving unconditional acceptance. It is a way of living that is secure not because of anything we have done, or have to keep doing, but purely because of God's love, which is totally dependable.

"Though the mountains may move and the hills shake, my love will be immoveable and never fail"
Isaiah 54:10b (REB)

Some peoples' response to this new experience of life is so dramatic that it involves the literal letting go of – *the stripping away of* – the trophies of the previous experience of life. For example St Francis of Assisi, in response to his discovery of God's Grace, gave away everything he possessed and lived entirely on the riches he found in being a son of God. To him the things we call 'success' were merely a burden, and a barrier to God.

But it is highly important that we don't misunderstand saints like Francis of Assisi. He did not give up his possessions in order to *receive* God's Grace. He gave them away as a wild and generous act of joyful abandonment in *response to* God's Grace.

God's Grace *always* precedes our actions. This is an important lesson. God's Grace is pre-existent. We can only *respond* to it. We can choose not to accept it, but we can never stop it from flowing.

Also, if we are going to try to apply St Francis' teachings to ourselves, we need to be realistic. I think most of us will end up living with the tension of having possessions but not being possessed by them. We should always seek to be grateful for what we have *without becoming attached*, and that's a hard lesson for the little-me.

And the same thing applies to other forms of success. Like for example our personal awards, achievements, medals, qualifications and so on. Of course these things are not bad or wrong. They are good. Indeed our academic qualifications are a sign of the level of our education, and are consequently necessary for further education or making a career. But to use them as badges of superiority that make you feel 'better' than those who don't have them, is to turn them sour. I've known people who seemed to be obsessed by the letters after their name. In fact I know some *Clergy* who seem to be more concerned about the letters that come *after* their name, than the ones that come *before* it. Of course neither make any difference to our inner core as a human being. They can be useful for saying something about our educational journey, but they can be down right dangerous if worn as badges of superiority.

I happened to train for the ministry at a theological college with a high number of students from a very academic background. It was a wonderful place to study, and I count it as a great privilege to have spent three years there. However on my first visit I noticed the names of the prospective students on a notice-board in the college hall. Our names had our academic titles set out alongside them. So we knew exactly who had what degree, doctorate etc., and who had nothing. Since I was one of the ones with nothing, I thought it would be funny to write my *highest* qualification alongside my name, so it read *Mark Townsend (O Level Art).*

It was silly and childish, but it does have a serious side because the system was comparing and making distinctions between people, and was creating a feeling among the students of first and second-rate ordinands. Some students even referred to the Diploma in Ministry (as opposed to the Degree course) as the 'dim' course.

To create a religion of achievements and successes, be they academic, religious, or even spiritual, is to fall into the trap of Pharisaism. The 'religion' of Christ is based not on our abilities but on God's Grace. I heard the following saying a few years ago: *'being a Christian is not our responsibility! It's our response to God's ability.'* Cheesy but true!

Yet do I listen to this teaching myself? Do I really understand it and act upon it? Here's another little extract from my journal, written in the Spring 2000. I was supposed to be writing a sermon about Pentecost and was letting out all my thoughts and feelings. It's interesting that this was only a few weeks before I was signed off work for six weeks with a course of anti-depressants and counselling. I had become 'success' oriented and was worn out by my own egotistical efforts at trying to be Revd. Perfect:

Why don't I listen to myself? What is it about me that refuses to apply to myself what I try to teach to others? 'Stop!' I say, 'take a break. Don't try so hard to achieve all those things in your own strength.' Am I really so stupid that I think it applies to everyone but me? My God, I get so tired being a perfectionist; trying to please; trying to achieve; trying to hold together all the contradictions and frustrations of a broad church. 'Hand it over to God' is maybe what I'd say to another. ***But what does that mean?*** *I guess it means to let go and to abandon oneself to the greater power. I guess it means to recognise, like the new Alcoholics Anonymous convert, that I can't do it alone but that a greater power is available that can and will help me.*

Pentecost is on its way. What a powerful symbol of the freeing of trust in the ego and the relaxing into the living power of God within. Yet people have distorted Pentecost into some struggle for spiritual supernatural self-attainment. Why can't we see that we 'get' because we 'give up' not because we 'grab'. The great antithesis of Pentecost is symbolized by the Hebrew myth of Babel. These two stories, Babel and Pentecost, both come up as readings for today, which is great for they both throw light on one another.

Babel was humanity's prideful attempt to build a tower and reach God by sheer self-effort. They may have ended up with a very successful monument of towering architecture but failed in their task to 'get' to God. All they achieved was a confusion of language resulting in gibberish and total disunity.

Pentecost, on the other hand, was God's power being sent freely, and dramatically 'down' upon a mass of people, who, though speaking all sorts of languages could actually understand one another. Thus we have a picture of UNITY as a result of God-power, as opposed to the Babel picture of DISUNITY due to people-power. Pentecost is a story about relying on God and not self.

If I had listened to my own teaching and put it into practice I may well have avoided the breakdown I suffered. But I didn't listen, and continued for some time striving and struggling in my own strength to be a 'successful priest'.

We are living a culture of success. We in the West are living in a culture where a person's value is calculated according to what he or she can produce. People are becoming expendable. When they slow down, or fail to achieve, they are valued less and less until they become 'value-less'.

Our culture is also individualistic and, though we are apparently no longer a class-conscious culture, is inadvertently creating a terrifying class divide between the 'successful' and the 'non-successful'. The frightening thing for me is that I see the Church buying into this culture, or scarier still, I see myself buying into it.

So what is a successful church? Well, let me see if I can paint a mental picture for you. Imagine a church that is financially secure, able to attract people of all ages, has an attendance of 300 on every Sunday and a regular praying body of 10-15 at the Daily Offices. It stands up for issues of morality and has worship services of musical perfection and liturgical beauty.

Yes, that might be a picture of a successful church, *but it could also be a spiritual failure*. Maybe this church is doing very well on the level of attracting people and paying its way, but does it have the capacity to bring people (inside and outside the community) into the all-embracing unconditional love of Christ? We must not just look at the apparent outward success and assume everything is rosy.

If we base our spirituality on outward success alone we will make the terrifying mistake that many made two Millennia ago in Palestine when outward appearances were all that mattered for the religious elite.

Jesus did *not* come to bring people success. He did not come to create a successful church. He did not come to make people respectable, or polite or drag them up the social class system. No, Jesus came for almost precisely the opposite reason – to make friends of the failures and the sinners.

'I did not come to call the virtuous, but sinners'
MATTHEW 9:13B (REB)

It was no accident that the very people who were open to the words Jesus spoke were generally not the successful (the rich) or the religious elite. The ones who were open to the words of the Gospel were the poor, the marginalized and the ritually imperfect and unclean (Mark 1:23-26; Matthew 8:2-3; Luke 4;18-19; John 9:1-7).

He even made a group of disciples out of twelve men who never stopped getting things wrong. Take some time to read the earliest Gospel, St Mark. It is amazing how patient Jesus is with these twelve clowns who just can't get it right.

John Fenton's wonderful book 'More about Mark', gives us a wonderful glimpse into the *necessity* of the disciples' failure and missing of the point:

It [Mark's Gospel] *is the best book for the twenty-first century because it is so utterly subversive. Western European culture will need some subversive people to do something about its capitalism and its love of self. The one character who is the model in Mark's Gospel is the child and the child is there as a representative of people who are unskilled, nobodies; who have no status. The child appears twice, in chapter 9 and in chapter 10, and in both cases, Jesus hugs them. They are the only people that he does hug. The rich will find it hard to enter the kingdom of God. The first will be last and the last will be first. Life will be through death; death will be the only way forward. This will be necessary for the twenty-first century, when what we will all be trying to do is live as long as possible and be as rich as possible. But notice one thing about this rich man: he wants to know what he should do. He has kept the commandments and Jesus says he lacks one thing – 'Sell what you have and give to the poor', and the man goes away sad. And it says there in Mark, 'Jesus looked at him and loved him'. It is the only instance of Jesus loving somebody. He loves the person who can't do it. This again is subversive and this is what is so good about Mark. He saw that his readers would never be able to accept his book, and he was right...*

...We see the impossibility of the demand, 'Destroy your life! That's the only way to preserve it.' And we know we can't do it, but the man who couldn't do it was the one that Jesus loved. Away success! Welcome failure! That's the good news.

[7] **John Fenton.**

When you really take time to think about it Jesus' ministry was not successful if viewed in terms of our current culture of success. He didn't end up with a 'super-church'. His tiny band of followers betrayed him. His messianic campaign ended up not with him being recognised as the answer to problems of his people but as *the problem itself.* He was not respected as the bringer of God's liberation, but was executed as a dangerous subversive and blasphemer. Success?

Jesus faced the ultimate 'failure' of losing his life in a most humiliating and despicable way. HE WAS NOT a success. And yet that is again precisely the point. Jesus turned everything on its head by allowing himself to lose everything – even his own life. He is the Messiah of the underdog, the rejected, the failure, the sinner, the unworthy, the lost, and the fallen.

And inside this failure and utter human tragedy, *IS* the success – the true success of the GOSPEL, for it is a Gospel *for the imperfect ones, which is all of us.* As John Fenton said, "Away success! Welcome failure! That is the good news."

Yet there has always been a dreadful religious quest for perfection, even among the followers of the crucified one.

CHAPTER SIX

OUR DREADFUL QUEST FOR PERFECTION

'In a Navajo rug there is always an imperfection woven into the corner. And interestingly enough, it's where "the Spirit moves in and out of the rug." The pattern is perfect and then there's one part of it that clearly looks like a mistake. The Semitic mind, the Eastern mind (which, by the way, Jesus would have been much closer to) understands perfection in precisely this way.

Perfection is not the elimination of imperfection. That's our Western either/or, need-to-control thinking. Perfection, rather, is the ability to incorporate imperfection! There's no other way to live: you either incorporate imperfection, or you fall into denial. That's how the Spirit moves in or out of our lives.'

[8] **Richard Rohr.**

'If a job's worth doing it's worth doing badly'.

I cannot remember where I came across the second of the above quotes but I do like it. No, actually I (the 'little-me') hate it! You see *I am* a perfectionist!

Many people see me as spontaneous, chilled out and laid back. But in reality I get so obsessed with wanting everything to be perfect that I make myself miserable and stressed. There is a horrific control freak inside me! Most perfectionists are control freaks. We really don't like anything to go wrong, and tiny, insignificant details can dominate out minds. We want everything to be perfect, and all potential hazards to be eliminated. And, because life isn't like that, we tend to be rather on edge. So we hate those wise-guy phrases like the above one, *yet need to learn their lesson so much.*

Perfectionists, and especially religious ones, feel they've always got to prove something. Those who've studied personality types will know that some perfectionists are people who grew up struggling to be noticed. They perhaps got very little attention as children, and when it came, it tended to be negative. They learned that in order to be noticed they had to escape from being the person they were by imitating others. They, consequently, grew up with a deep dissatisfaction with their own personality, and an inner need to change, which was a great emotional pressure for them.

There are also perfectionists who grew up as 'Master or Miss Goodie Two Shoes'; the one son or daughter in the family who never puts a foot wrong, like Perfect Peter in the children's *Horrid Henry* books. They were likely to take this character to school too, where they would probably have become the teacher's pet. They also grew up under pressure; pressure to keep up the image, for they knew that if they were to put a foot wrong they'd be in more trouble than the ones who were expected to be naughty. They were the ones who the adults relied upon to maintain their perfection, as an example to the rest. The poor things would know that, should they ever fail, they would be likely to hear these words spoken from an adult's mouth, 'Oh how *you*'ve let *me* down'.

In time the children who feel they need to be *different* to get adult attention, and the children who feel they need to be *good* to get adult approval, project all that crap onto God, and He becomes the unsatisfied and disapproving parent/teacher par-excellence.

This is a bold statement that some might find difficult, but perfectionism is like an addiction or an obsessive compulsion, and often needs to be treated as such. Perfectionists think, "I have to do this myself, or it will never be done properly", so the desire to be in control takes over and letting go becomes almost impossible. An addiction is anything you are *not* free *not* to do, so the intense *need* to be in control is highly addictive behaviour. In my opinion many clergy are perfectionists and control freaks. But of course it's not entirely our fault. There has been an unhealthy 'need' for the laity to have perfect priests and clergy too.

The fact is, no, not just the fact, but the life-enriching truth is that (clergy or not) we can all be shits *but God loves us anyway*. In fact he thinks we are so fantastic that he became one of us. And what's more God's love for us, in our shitty state, was so un-conditional that it killed Him. God, in human form, *loved us to death,* ***literally!*** He even forgave the very ones who had hammered those terrifying nails into his hands and feet: 'Father, forgive them; they do not know what they are doing.' (Luke 23:34 REB).

Could one imagine a more grievous and blasphemous crime than to spit on and beat and kill the Son of God? Yet he forgives them in the very act of committing this crime. Amazing! There is only forgiveness in this God, no violence at all, not even ritual violence dished out upon an innocent victim on our behalf.

I realise the previous statement is controversial, but I simply do not buy the notion that Jesus died absorbing God's wrathful punishment on our behalf. I know it is what the church so often teaches, but I see Jesus' death more in terms of a costly and loving declaration and revelation of how all-embracing, and unconditional God's love is, *and always was*. Christ died a violent death not at the hands of a violent God, but a violent humanity.

It was not God's opinion of us that changed through the cross, but the possibility of our opinion of Him changing.

On that note I thoroughly recommend the startling books *Knowing Jesus* and *On Being Liked*, by theologian James Alison, if you want to discover a profoundly liberating new way of viewing the violence of the cross.

Of course, no matter how much I believe in a God who loves me as I am I know I will always have a little perfectionist inside me. It's part of who I am, and to want things to be done to the best of one's ability is hardly wrong. The problem is not with wanting to do the best one can but with the thought that our personal value and self worth is somehow tied up with it.

What we need in order to loosen the grip of unhealthy perfectionism in our lives is a continual journey of conversion to the Gospel of Grace! A continual exposure to Unconditional Love. Experience has taught me that conversion is a *constant process* rather than a once and for all 'bolt from the blue'. I know that every so often I get another glimpse of this wild and outrageous gift of God's Grace, but within days lose sight of it again as I try to achieve the next goal.

How does this conversion happen? Indeed what is conversion? Well, here we enter controversial waters again, for I think that conversion is not something we opt for or even try to make happen, but something that *happens to us*. I want us to look for a while at a very well known Biblical parable, which is for me *the text* for the

Gospel of Falling Down. I believe it demonstrates how an apparent fall *from* Grace was really a fall *into* Grace. I believe that this parable gives us a picture of the true heart of God, and of two different 'types' of religious response. Ironically the one who falls finds, and the one who already has, cannot see *what* he has. It shows us how mere religious rule-keeping and doing things by the book can lead to spiritual blindness, whereas 'falling' can lead to true enlightenment. Failure can expose us to Grace. So let's look again at Jesus' beautiful story of the failure who has become known to us as the Prodigal Son.

CHAPTER SEVEN

THE LOST SON(S)

O God will I ever be first?

I began to come to you, but I found you coming to me.

I wanted to run to you, but I found you running to me.

I wanted to wait for you, but I found you waiting for me.

I wanted to search for you, but I found you searching for me.

I thought I found you, but was found by you.

I wanted to say 'I love you', but heard you say 'I love you'.

I wanted to choose you, but you have chosen me.

I wanted to write to you, but I received your letter.

I wanted to live in you, but I found you living in me.

I wanted to ask your forgiveness, but I found you forgiving me.

I wanted to offer myself to you, but I found you offering yourself to me.

I wanted to offer friendship to you, but I found you offering your friendship to me.

I wanted to call you 'Abba Father', but I heard you calling 'My Son' first.

I wanted to reveal my inner life to you, but I found you offering your inner life to me.

I wanted to invite you into my life, but I received your invitation into your life.

I wanted to rejoice over my return, but found you rejoicing over my return.

O God, WILL I EVER BE FIRST?

[9] **Brother John Martin Sahajananda.**

If there was one of Jesus' parables that could be called the Parable of the Gospel of Falling Down, it would be the following:

THE LOST SON

There was once a man who had two sons. The younger one said to him, 'Father, give me my share of the property now.' So the man divided his property between his two sons. After a few days the younger son sold his part of the property and left home with the money. He went to a country far away, where he wasted his money by reckless living. He spent everything he had. Then a severe famine spread over that country, and he was left without a thing. So he went to work for one of the citizens of that country, who sent him out to his farm to take care of the pigs. He wished he could fill himself with the bean pods the pigs ate, but no one gave him anything to eat. At last he came to his senses and said, 'All my father's hired workers have more than they can eat, and here I am about to starve! I will get up and go to my father and say, father I have sinned against God and against you. I am no longer fit to be called your son; treat me as one of your hired workers.' So he got up and started back to his father.

He was still a long way from home when his father saw him; his heart was filled with pity, and he ran, threw his arms round his son, and kissed him. 'Father,' the son said, 'I have sinned against God and against you. I am no longer fit to be called your son.' But the father called his servants. 'Hurry!' he said. 'Bring the best robe and put it on him. Put a ring on his finger and shoes on his feet.

Then go and get the prize calf and kill it, and let us celebrate with a feast! For this son of mine was dead, but now he is alive; he was lost, but now he has been found. And so the feasting began.

In the meantime the elder son was out in the field. On his way back, when he came close to the house, he heard the music and dancing. So he called one of the servants and asked him, 'What's going on?' 'Your brother has come back home,' the servant answered, 'and your father has killed the prize calf, because he got him back safe and sound.'

The elder brother was so angry that he would not go into the house; so his father came out and begged him to come in. But he answered his father, 'Look, all these years I have worked for you like a slave, and I have never disobeyed your orders. What have you given me? Not even a goat for me to have a feast with my friends! But this son of yours wasted all your property on prostitutes, and when he comes back home, you kill the prize calf for him!' 'My son,' the father answered, 'you are always here with me, and everything I have is yours. But we had to celebrate and be happy, because your brother was dead, but now he is alive; he was lost, but now he has been found.'

Luke 15:11-32 (GNB/CEV)

This is one of the most startling stories ever told. I never tire of hearing it. It still has the capacity to move me to tears. You can taste the emotional depth of the situation. You can feel the power of transforming Grace penetrate the soul of the lost son as he melts in his father's welcoming arms.

But is it really a story about a Lost Son? Of course it *is* a story about a boy who runs away from home with half his dad's inheritance, wastes it all, falls flat on his face ending up spiritually and socially lost, and some time later returns. But I want to suggest that this is a story about *two lost sons,* and when we start to see *two* lost son-characters we begin to recognise two types of religious behaviour. Most people tend to see this story as a testimony of an evangelical repentance/conversion. *Yet it is so much more than that.* I believe that this story shows us the paradox between the person who does it all wrong, and yet finds freedom and Grace, and the person who does it all right, yet remains spiritually blind and unenlightened.

I also think that this story gives us a little insight into the unpopular theme of judgement.

There are three main characters in this little story; a father and his two sons. One of the two sons asks for his share of inheritance and leaves home. He leaves home because he wants to experience life. He certainly has all the security he needs with his father, but that's clearly not enough. He seems bored and longs for stimulation. Notice that the father is *not* possessive. He does not cling to the boy pleading with him to stay, nor does he allow himself to be offended and angrily send him off without his blessing. He simply *allows* him to leave. Thus the first deep insight into the nature of God comes right here at the very beginning of the story. God is not an over protective parent. He knows that for some of his children leaving home for a while is a necessary experience even if it ends in *Falling Down.* Leaving home may well be leaving the religion that a young person's parents have struggled so hard to bring him or her up within. It is *any* experience that in the end teaches the seeker that what they are looking for cannot be found out there but is waiting back at home. The *irony* is that they would never find it *without* first going through the painful period of leaving home.

I began this book with a story about an egg of gold. There is a type of fairy tale/myth where the heroes and heroines have to go on some great quest for treasure. The treasure they discover is the wisdom that comes from the voyage itself, and that wisdom enables them to return to where they came from and uncover the treasure that was *there all along.*

A short version of this myth is the Rabbi's Gold, which is a story about a very poor Polish Rabbi who dreams of hidden treasure. He travels to the place of the treasure but cannot dig it up because of a fact beyond his control. However he meets a man there who tells him how he dreamed of a particular Rabbi who lived on top of hidden treasure. Well of course the Rabbi raced back home and uncovered the treasure that was indeed buried under his own roof.

If you have not already read it, another beautiful story based on this theme is the enchanting novel *The Alchemist*, by Paulo Coelho.

There are many such stories in the folklore of every culture. They clearly point to a universal truth; that the greatest treasure we will ever discover is found not 'out there' but back at home, yet is often only truly discovered after the failure of the original quest to find it.

The journey made by the prodigal son is a quest for a particular kind of life satisfaction where such 'life satisfaction' can never be found. He sought adventure and stimulation, and for a while it was fun and gave a certain amount of pleasure, but like any compulsive behaviour it cannot last, *and will turn sour.* When his money ran out his luck also ran out, and so did his enjoyment of life. He soon discovered the consequences of looking for happiness in the wrong places. He began to suffer, but not because of any external judgement. The suffering was coming not from a wrathful father figure. His father was apparently still looking out, longingly searching the horizon with wide opens arms and Grace-filled eyes. No, the boy's suffering was a direct consequence of his quest to find meaning in the wrong place.

Many Christians would assume that a person in this state was now well and truly under the judgement and wrath of God, especially considering he had not yet repented. But when we study this story with care, can we see *any* element of judgement in the father figure? All I see is a loving and forgiving dad waiting for his son to fall back into his open arms.

The story says how the son 'came to his senses', but it's important that we also recognise that he had actually assumed his father would not receive him back as a son. As the reality of his predicament struck him with full force, he suddenly remembered his home, and the fact that life as a servant back there was so much better than life for him in the here and now. He knew what he would have to do, but expected no more than to be allowed to live as a servant (and perhaps he would not even be given that privilege).

He was ready to say to his father, 'I am no longer fit to be called your son. Treat me as one of your hired workers'. Clearly this boy *did not expect to receive forgiveness and a second chance.* One could even question whether he really *knew* his father's heart at all. He was imagining that his father was harbouring judgement, even resentment, against him. He was *projecting* his own self-judgement onto his father. How interesting!

How many of us have felt God's judgement? I think I have –

time and time again. As I've pointed out, it's all the way through my journal. But no, wait a minute, that was my little-me speaking. Maybe *that* is what judgement is? Could it be that God has given us the capacity to feel guilt (self-judgement) but that He himself holds no such judgement against us – *EVER?* That is a *question* for you to consider, not a statement of fact! But it would seem that in the case of this story, the father (God) held no wrath and no judgement toward the boy, *even before he shows signs of repentance.*

In fact let's take this one step further. Did the son repent at all? The fact is we don't really know what his heart was doing as he 'came to his senses'. He certainly knew what words he would have to speak, "I have sinned against heaven and against you…" but was this because he had really repented? One thing we *can* say is that the forgiveness (and I would say the redemption) was *already flowing before* the son had a chance to get his words out. The normal evangelical understanding of a person receiving redemption is that it *follows* a person's repentance. The sinner turns and confesses his/her sin and in response, God forgives and thus redeems. But does it sometimes happen the other way round? Is our repentance sometimes a response to the redemption we have already freely received and experienced?

My own particular belief about this story is that it demonstrates God's totally unconditional love and forgiveness that flows ceaselessly in our direction. The son running into his father's arms was met by such mind-blowing Grace and love that he melted. His repentance was in response to the redemption he was being offered. He had found what he *didn't even know he was looking for*, and certainly didn't expect to receive.

He was indeed dead, and alive again.

My goodness, if only we could truly hold on to that awesome picture of God as the father of the lost son. How our lives would be transformed. When we have a judgemental view of God, we spend our lives trying to change and be accepted. However, when we meet the God of Unconditional Love we don't *have* to try any more, and yet find transformation happening naturally.

Earlier on I said this story is not about a lost son, but *two* lost sons. So let's look again at the narrative of the older brother.

The older brother was so angry that he would not go into the house; so his father came out and begged him to come in. But he answered his father, 'Look, all these years I have worked for you like a slave, and I have never disobeyed your orders. What have you given me? Not even a goat for me to have a feast with my friends! But this son of yours wasted all your property on prostitutes, and when he comes back home, you kill the prize calf for him!'

First of all let's not be too harsh on this poor soul! After all, his anger is quite understandable. His position is similar to that of the workers in the vineyard from another of Jesus' parables. These men had worked all day for a good wage, but at pay time realised that they would have got the same amount whatever time they had begun their work, for even the workers who had only just started work got the same. (Matthew 20:1-16).

So the anger in all these characters, whether the older brother or the workers, is not due to the father or boss being unjust and ungenerous, but to the fact that he didn't differentiate between those who worked harder (and for longer) and those who didn't. Again, this points to the father heart of God that does not reward according to what a person has achieved but according to who they are, a human being made in the image of God. Meritocracy is the way of the world, but it is not the way of God. These parables are uncomfortable precisely because they do not fit in with our expectations of wanting it all to be fair and 'tit for tat'. We want God to be like us, rewarding those who work the hardest, but God offers the same gift to everyone, whether they deserve it or not.

The sad irony when it comes to the older son is that, though he is still offered the same gift, he refuses to receive it and symbolically places himself in exactly the same position as his brother had been, out there with the pigs.

This is quite an amazing picture. The one who is morally in the right, who has been a 'good boy', and stayed in his father's house without straying to the left or to the right, has ended up denying himself what he is being freely offered. Look at it this way, his *perfectionism* has become a *barrier* to Grace, whereas the younger son's *imperfection* has become a *channel* into the experience of Grace.

The older son reminds me of the folk that every church has its share of; those who are so perfect, and holy, and law abiding that they ooze not Grace but a very unattractive self-righteousness and puritanical severity. We *all* have the capacity to be like that. The poor older son is an image of the part of each one of us that wants to earn God's love and approval; the part of us that is perfectionist, moralistic, and self-righteous. The amazing thing about this story is that the righteous one ended up further away from the Gospel than the one who committed almost every sin in the book. But *that* is very often the way in the Bible. There is a clear theme within scripture that stresses the strange notion that the ones who make mistakes, who are failures, even sinners, are closer to the kingdom of God than the righteous. The fallen ones in scripture seem to have a spiritual advantage over those who were religiously perfect.

Jesus once declared to the Chief Priests and elders of the temple in Jerusalem:

"I tell you solemnly, tax collectors and prostitutes are making their way into the kingdom of God before you. For John came to you, a pattern of true righteousness, but you did not believe him, and yet the tax collectors and prostitutes did."

Matthew 21:31a-32a (Jerusalem Bible)

On another occasion this little discussion occurred on a similar theme:

...he [Jesus] noticed a tax collector, Levi by name, sitting by the customs house, and he said to him, "Follow me". And leaving everything he got up and followed him.

In his honour Levi held a great reception in his house, and with them at the table was a large gathering of tax collectors and others. The Pharisees and their scribes complained to his disciples and said, "Why do you eat and drink with tax collectors and sinners?" Jesus said to them in reply, "It is not those who are well who need the doctor, but the sick. I have not come to call the virtuous, but sinners to repentance".

Mark 2:14-17

In some strange way the sinner seems to be in a better position to hear about the transforming gift of Grace than the righteous. It is as if the very fact of recognising one's sins, flaws, imperfections and cracks, opens one up to what a 'perfect' vessel can never fully experience because there is no wound through which the Grace can flow.

The next chapter is based on a presentation that I saw a remarkable biblical scholar called Frances Young give. It was during a conference on St Paul's Second Letter to the Corinthians and was a profound experience.

I asked Professor Young if I could have a copy of her presentation and adapt it for use on my retreat. The full presentation will constitute the first part of Chapter Eight of this book.

AN EXERCISE:

(BASED ON AN ANALOGY FROM FR ANTHONY DE MELLO)

Find yourself a piece of string and a pair of scissors.

Now hold the string by one end and let it let it drop vertically.

(Fig 10)

Imagine that this string represents our relationship with God.

It's not ideal because it seems to suggest that God is 'up there' and we are 'down here' but for our purposes it will suffice!

OK, now cut it in the middle.

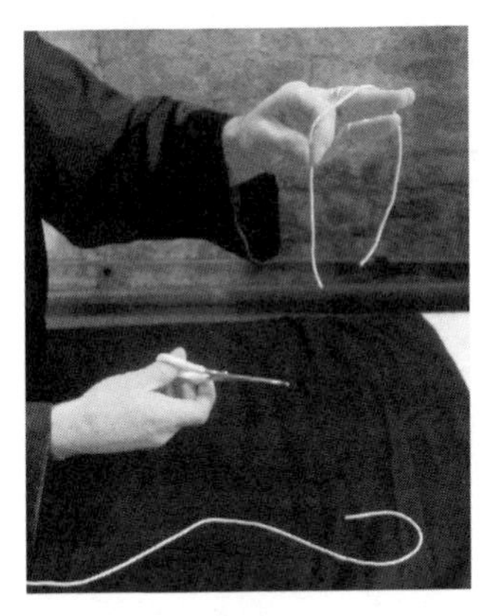

(Fig 11)

This snip of the scissors represents a 'sin', which breaks the relationship. Watch the lower half of the string fall to the ground. Feel the isolation – the separation – that the action has caused. Think of something that you have done, said or thought that has left you feeling separate and broken like this string.

Now tie the two pieces back together with a knot, and repair the string. See your hands now as God's hands, for He always repairs the relationship, and heals brokenness.

Observe the repaired string – the restored relationship. See how God's hands picked up the fallen piece and grafted it back onto to the other piece. Redemption comes from God, all we need to be is willing and open to allow him to pick us back up.

Now perform the same actions again. Cut the string, watch it fall, and repair the brokenness. Do this a few times.

Through our lives we keep falling, and momentarily wounding the relationship with God, but just as fast as we 'cut' the string God is busy picking it back up and repairing it.

Now after many cuts and repairs with knots, hold up the string once more.

(Fig 12)

Look! Observe that the string has got shorter, thus bringing the two ends closer together. So, our sins, by some strange irony, momentarily break our relationship with God, but then bring us closer to God than we were before the break.

Reflect on this image and allow the healing power of God's Grace to be a reality for you. Bask for a while in the wonder and glory of God's unconditional love.

CHAPTER EIGHT

THE TREASURE AND THE CLAY

'Life is too important to be wasted in yearning to be rich, famous, good looking, popular, or pretty, or in dreading being poor, unknown, ignored, or ugly. These things become unimportant, as though they were pebbles alongside a dazzling diamond. You – your true self – have always been and will always be a diamond.'

[10] **Anthony de Mello.**

There are various 'props' for this presentation. As you read it you will notice that I have set out in brackets what these props are, and what they do. I have also introduced a *magic* element into it. Try to imagine the object lessons as you read the script.

[The participants are sitting in a semi-circle. On the floor is a large mat on which is an object that has been entirely covered by a big black cloth. I am kneeling down by the side of the object]

The Bible begins in vast empty *darkness.* Nothing – no matter, and certainly no light. But God, whose words speak reality into being, said 'Let there be light', and there was light. Light that chased away the darkness.

[The black cloth is whipped away and placed out of sight. It reveals a large Middle Eastern clay jar]

(Fig 13)

Some time later He hung two *lamps* in the sky. We now call them the sun and the moon.

Ancient lamps looked something like this…

[I pass round a lamp for all to see]

(Fig 14)

I made this with some modelling terracotta. Biblical lamps would have been simple, and made from baked clay. They would have had a wick, and would be filled with oil.

So, light, light that was used by these Biblical folk to chase away the darkness, was held in clay vessels.

God used clay Himself in the next story of the Bible. Yes He scooped up a clump of earth and moulded it into the form of a man.

Clay figurines were very common in the ancient Near East.

Again, I had a go at making one. It's not very good, but it gives us an idea of what they might have looked like...

[I hand out a clay person]

(Fig 15)

But God doesn't just mould a man-shaped piece of clay, He breathes into it, He breathes *His life* into it.

So Biblically speaking, both light, *the light of God*, and life, *the life of God* is contained within clay pots and figures.

St Paul spoke of 'treasure in jars of clay'. I wonder, was he getting his inspiration from these earlier creation stories where God's light and God's life is held inside such fragile items as clay lamps and figurines?

By the time of the New Testament, of course, such pots were more than common. They were used for storing all sorts of things, from water, grain and oil to more precious things like money…

[I take some gold coins from the jar and throw them onto the mat]

…valuables and precious treasures…

[I take from the jar some golden necklaces, and then some beads and precious stones, placing them all on the mat]

...holy scrolls...

[Now about twenty or thirty rolled up parchments are taken out of the jar and given out to the people]

Remember the great discovery of the Dead Sea Scrolls? Those sacred texts were preserved because they had been kept within large clay jars.

So it was literally true that in the Ancient Near East ordinary clay jars *did* indeed hold extraordinary hidden treasures within.

It is also metaphorically true that we have our treasure close at hand, within the humble shell of a jar made of clay. *Not* at the end of some holy quest, or knightly expedition, but here, in the present moment, now, within this very physical location and reality.

And what is this treasure that we already possess? Gold, silver, books? *NO!, Light and Life,* the Light and Life of God.

And where are the jars? They are here, in this room, for each one of us is a clay jar; a clay jar that contains priceless jewels.

Clay pots and jars are a perfect analogy for the human body, especially in Biblical times, and in the developing world today, because, like clay jars, human bodies and human lives are fragile. But *we* in the modern West have lost something of the sense of the human body and human life being fragile and imperfect. Some of us have even begun to think that human bodies should be outwardly perfect in a way that they never can be. We are more and more being encouraged to make them into what magazine images or other myths from popular culture say they should be like.

Different forms of perfectionism are all around us, even in religions, *especially* in the Church.

The sad fact is that much religion has simply missed the point. For the great spiritual traditions have always taught that our intrinsic value has nothing to do with either our outer appearance *or* our external achievements. Our value comes from the fact that we are made in the image and likeness of God, and that we may well be like fragile clay jars, but we contain within our own frail yet beautiful humanity the precious gift of God's Light and Life. Our essential core of being *IS GOD!*

Millions of good, devout religious people have been encouraged to set our focus on great external achievements and goals which we were told will bring us value and worth, and make us more Christ-like. But, metaphorically speaking, this has often led us down the path of trying to change our God given clay jars into human made 'golden vessels'.

And we simply cannot do this, and if we try then our efforts won't last for long. We cannot manufacture our own Christ-like-ness by pure ego-effort. We may be able to turn ourselves into the model Christian, and he or she may look lovely for a while, but it will be largely counterfeit. And sooner or later it will start to crack and splinter. Remember that the people that gave Jesus the hardest time were those who had successfully changed themselves into what religion said they should be like. Something needed to happen to them to make them open to the gift of God's Grace. They needed to come down from their ivory towers of self-righteousness and fall – *yes fall* – into the hands of the one they were resisting.

He could have caught them, and then taught them (like He did so many others) that they already have the inner treasure of God and do not need to try and earn it or attain it by religious perfectionism. By trying to earn it they only prolonged the discovery of it.

So, let me now show you the great mystery and miracle of the *Gospel of Falling Down.* We are beautifully and intricately designed clay jars, fashioned lovingly by a wonderful Creator. Yet, we are also fragile and poor. And from time to time life causes us to splinter and crack.

Life may dish out something totally beyond our control, something we would have never asked for, something 'out of the blue'. *Or* it may be that we have walked for a while the road of the Pharisee and tried to make ourselves into little icons of religious perfection. Maybe we have fallen flat on our faces after the painful discovery that such a goal is impossible. Maybe our failure to achieve a goal has triggered a humiliating fall leading to the recognition of our limitations and weaknesses. This falling of the clay jar has wounded us and we have started to crack and splinter.

These cracks and splinters (whichever way they came) are painful, horribly painful; even like death. Yet if only we knew how close we were in this state to the discovery of our lifetime.

For when we fall, and splinter and crack, we see our ego, our false self, our little-me, for what it is, and sometimes (just sometimes) we are able to let go of it for a while. Then the most profound experience is waiting to hit us. You see, the crack, the fault, the brokenness exposes THE INNER TREASURE AT LAST!!!

[At this point I slowly turn round the clay jar (out of which all those coins and paper scrolls have come) to reveal a huge crack in the other side. And due to the fact that there is a hidden large burn-

ing candle inside the jar the light pours out through the crack for all to see.]

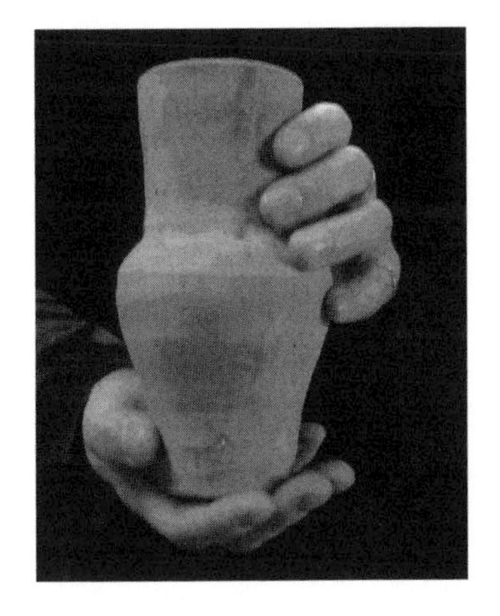

(Fig 16 and Fig 17)

And then we can truly say that we have met God, and have met Him not out there at the end of some great quest but within our very selves. The treasure that we were searching for *out there* is finally re-discovered.

And know this; the treasure is not something that has been suddenly added to our selves, for it was always there. Rather it is our perception that has changed, our 'inner eyesight'. That's why people often say spirituality is about 'seeing'.

Of course this doesn't happen automatically. It may be months or even years after our fall that we see ourselves in our own God-given-glory. We may be so hurt by our fall that we grow bitter, and again close ourselves to our inner beauty and treasure.

But make no mistake, such falls, and the cracks they produce, *can* indeed give us the sacred opportunity to catch a golden glimpse of the God-self.

I want to close this chapter with a lovely Chinese fable.

THE CRACKED POT

A water bearer in China had two large pots. Each hung on the ends of a pole, which he carried across his neck. One pot had a crack in it, while the other pot was perfect and always delivered a full portion of water. At the end of the long walk from the stream to the house, the cracked pot arrived only half full.

For a full two years this went on daily, with the bearer delivering only one and a half pots full of water to his house. Of course, the perfect pot was proud of its accomplishments, perfect for which it was made. But the poor cracked pot was ashamed of its own imperfection, and miserable that it was able to accomplish only half of what it had been made to do.

After two years of what it perceived to be bitter failure, it spoke to the water bearer one day by the stream... "I am ashamed of myself, because this crack in my side causes water to leak out all the way back to your house."

The bearer said to the pot, "Have you not noticed that there are flowers only on your side of the path, but not on the other pot's side?" That's because I have always known about your flaw, and I planted flower seeds on your side of the path. Every day while we walk back, you water them. For two years I have been able to pick these beautiful flowers to decorate the table. "Without you being just the way you are, there would not be this beauty to grace the house."

Anonymous

CHAPTER NINE

THE ROCK AT THE BOTTOM

A man went looking for the meaning of life. He passed through forests and over mountains and across seas. He talked to people along the way. All the while he was looking and listening, desperate for a clue to the deepest puzzle. Sometimes he thought he was on to it. He would follow up hints of mystery and words of wonder with mounting excitement and anticipation. But always he was disappointed. The promise of meaning would dissolve like wood smoke in the air. Many of the people he trusted turned out to be tricksters or merchants. In sadness he finally accepted that there was no meaning to life at all. The man took himself to the middle of a great bridge spanning a river gorge, intending to jump into the chasm. He couldn't even think of any message to leave. So he simply jumped. Instead of being smashed on the rocks below, he found himself caught in a pair of arms strong enough to break his fall. 'Who are you?' asked the man of his catcher. 'I'm the one who's been looking for you,' came the reply.

[11] **Mike Riddell.**

It seems there is a 'three steps forward, two steps back' tendency when it comes to the spiritual life. Or perhaps it's only me who has the capacity of missing the point just as quickly as getting it. Time and time again I go through the experience of being *spiritually cracked open*, as described in the previous chapter, which though painful, brings with it the possibility of catching another glimpse of the inner gold. Yet, try as I might, I cannot seem to hold on to the experience for long. All too often I find myself drifting back into precisely the same activity or pattern of behaviour that caused the eventual cracking in the first place. I simply forget my own teaching, the perfectionist within me rears his compulsive head again, and off I go climbing the rungs of the *ladder of perfection*... (until I can climb no further and fall off again). And so the cycle continues.

Somehow there ought to be a way of *staying with the treasure*.

The treasure itself, the inner gold, is found deep within our true selves. So it cannot be found at the top of a great metaphorical ladder, which is a spiritual climbing away from who we truly are. No, the gold comes after we have collapsed again into the true, honest, human and frail selves we find at the bottom of the ladder. The bottom is the place of discovery; it is where we 'come to our senses'. Interestingly, that is the precise phrase used of the Prodigal Son when he hit rock bottom; 'He came to his senses'. He could suddenly see. He could see that he'd been looking for the answer in the wrong place. He'd been walking away from himself, and from his own treasure. It was not an easy place to end up. He certainly would have felt shit, beaten up by life, and more than a little bit humiliated, yet there was also suddenly hope.

Rock bottom is an illuminating term to use for the place at the bottom of the ladder. In a recent episode of one of the UK's favourite soap operas, one character said to a young girl (who'd apologised for all the hell she'd caused), 'you've hit rock bottom love, so now the only way you can go is up!'

In other words you can't fall further than the hitting of that rock. It is there that the fall breaks. But there is something else too. A rock is solid ground. A rock will not collapse. A rock is a place on which you can actually build. I find that an amazing thought, we cannot build in thin air, yet so many of us try to. We can only truly build from the solid and honest place of the rock at the bottom – the place where *we are who we are.*

I believe that the rock on which we fall is sacred because it opens us up to God's love in a way that our climbing and achieving cannot. The reason this happens is quite simple. When we have fallen, cracked open and had everything stripped away, we momentarily see ourselves as we truly are, without all the layers, the grades, the achievements, the badges of honour, and the hats we wear. In this place status means nothing. We become naked, vulnerable, even ashamed, and at first it feels like death. In this place we can no longer rely on the *layers* for they are shown up for what they are, precisely nothing. But the amazing thing is that, though it can feel as though we have died, we are ironically more likely to hear the voice of the Divine Me in this place, because the little-me is associated with all those layers.

What follows is a dialogue between the *two voices* after hitting rock bottom. It might sound over dramatic, but I had got myself extremely worked up over something and felt like a hopeless failure.

'I want to die. Everything's lost. I can't believe I've been so stupid and let my guard down. God, I am a waste of time, a pathetic little shit who just can't do anything right. Why the hell do

you bother with me?'

'Keep talking Mark'.

'I just wanted to do it right God, I wanted to have what other people have, what other clergy have, a little bit of respect! Why don't people trust me? I'm not a threat to anyone. Why do they seem to despise me so much? Why do those people keep making me feel like I'll never be good enough for them? All I can see now is bloody darkness. Who the hell am I God?'

'You are Mark and I love you'.

'But who is Mark?'

'Mark' is simply the name your parents gave you. But your problem is that you confuse the Mark that you want to be (and try so hard to be) with the one who you already are. Now if you really want me to answer your question, 'But who is Mark?' then allow me to lead you somewhere in your imagination and trust me.

'I'll try.'

'No, too much trying is your problem Mark. For once let go of your controlling nature and allow yourself to be taken on a journey. All you need to be is open.

Mark, I am going to take you to a place that you may have heard about, but you might not recognise. I am going to take you to meet yourself. Just let me lead your thoughts…

You are falling… you are falling into a dark abyss.'

'I'm already there.'

'Don't talk Mark; just let me lead your thoughts. As you fall you see the clothes you've been wearing begin to split and tear at the seams. Your priest's clothing is in tatters, the beautiful vestments are now rags. But you notice that there are other

clothes now appearing on your body in their place. You can see the academic gown and colourful university hood you wore when you sat with your proud family to receive your degree. But now they are ripped and shredded and flung off into space.

As you keep falling more and more clothes appear, and are then in tatters. Clothes from work, combats from the Royal Marine selection weekend, school and scout uniforms, and all the clothes you wore as you went through all those fashion fads, like punk rock bondage suits, teddy boy style drapes and drainpipes, hippy afghan coats still smelling of patchouli, and the various costumes from all the martial arts clubs you've belonged to. They are all now in fragments as you are left still falling and totally naked.

Suddenly there is a thud as your fall is broken. You manage to stand up and look at yourself – battered, bruised and nude. You feel more vulnerable than ever before and try to work out who on earth you are for you cannot seem to remember anything. All the things you have ever done are now just a distant memory. All those achievements, experiences, and interests that have given you your identity are no more. You try to grasp at some of the labels you've applied to yourself but nothing comes. You feel frightened, disorientated and alone.'

'Oh God this is not helping'

'Quiet Mark, and trust me. Come back to the imaginative exercise. Because of the emotional intensity of the falling experience you feel exhausted and lie down. Before you know it you are asleep. Watch yourself sleeping Mark. Look at how peaceful your sleep is. You have just been through an experience like nothing before, but you have no bad memories to keep your

mind buzzing. For once your over active mind is still. You are sleeping like a baby sleeps. Now watch yourself wake up. You rise and discover yourself in a beautiful garden. The sleep has been good for you, but because of the stripping away of all your labels and layers you don't really know who you are.

'Oh God stop now, this is NOT helping. I asked you to show me who I am, not make me more confused by conjuring up imaginative fantasies about my amnesia'.

'You will soon discover who you are Mark, just trust and be led. You walk past a gorgeous tree full of the most exquisite fruit you've ever seen before, and you notice a little pathway, which you decide to follow. You walk on a hundred yards or so to a lovely pond, and you can see fish swimming near the surface that seem to have golden coloured backs. You peer in to take a closer look and can see your own reflection. It is you but a 'you' that you have never seen before. You seem so alive, and though you know the fish are gold coloured you distinctly see the glimmer of gold in your own reflection. You can't help but smile and your smile brightens the whole of the surface of the pond.

Then you stop, for across the pond you catch a glimpse of someone else. As you look at her she seems familiar but you can't place her. Is it your mother that she reminds you of, or you sister, or your daughter, or is it that woman from the superstore who served you last weekend? You look again and the crazy thing is that she reminds you of all of them... in fact of every woman and girl you know. And then she calls out to you, 'Hello Adam'.

'Who? Why the hell did she call me Adam?'

'Not hell Mark, but heaven, for this is how it was before hell was let loose inside the human mind.

Mark, this is who you truly are. Adam – before the fall – is your inner self. Adam is every man, and Eve is every woman. Their story is your story. Their sin was not stealing fruit but wanting to become what they were not. Mark, I have created a mechanism for coming back to who you truly are. Adam fell from grace, but your falls can be into grace if you allow them to be.'

'Oh God, are you telling me that when I fall, and can no longer rely on my labels, that I can become like Adam and Eve, before they were cast out of the garden?'

'Adam and Eve still exist Mark. They exist within all people, and they still live outside the garden. You live outside Eden. I tried to bring you all back into the garden when I came as the Second Adam, but you misunderstood my teaching and built another system that keeps people separate from me. Mark there is a way back to the garden – where you will see your inner gold – and it is to simply trust in me. Trust me when I say that I love you as you are. Do you realise, Mark, that you only fall because you need to fall? And you only need to fall because you always want to run away from your true self. You are obsessed with climbing up to where you think you should be. The falling is simply the way everything corrects itself.

'I still don't get this. I hate falling. It hurts and makes me feel like dying. I want to be well thought of, special, loved and valued. I try to be what I try to be because I am not content with the shit that I am. I want to achieve. I want to be a good priest. I want to feel respected. I want to be loved.'

'And you will never achieve any of those dreams if you keep on avoiding who you really are by climbing that ladder. Mark, listen to this: you cannot achieve these things because you

already have them. You are already loved by a force greater than anything. You are special Mark, as is every other person who lives. And if you stayed for longer in the place where you can see how special you are, then the changes you so deserve will come about naturally, rather than in a manufactured way.

Look once more Mark, at that person by the side of the pond in the garden. It IS you. He is the you that I created and who still exists inside and under all those layers of your complicated personality. You will never remove all those layers, nor should you try, for they have brought great lessons of their own. But when you do fall again, remember to look out for the one with the golden smile – HE IS THERE AND HE IS YOU. And my dream for you Mark, is that as time goes on you will need less falls, and will be able to spend longer with the gold.'

I am still in awe of that conversation. I make no claims that it was between me and God. Rather, I see it as a conversation between the two voices – the Divine Me and the little-me. I also confess that not all of it makes sense to me yet, but I thought it necessary to print as an example of how the rock at the bottom can be a place where the Divine Me is easier to hear.

However, it must be said that there are those who fall, and yet do not find it a place of discovery. For some it is simply too painful, and it will take literally years to begin to pick up all the pieces. For others their *little-me* is quite honestly so powerful and controlling that they immediately try to shift the blame for the fall elsewhere, and because of their humiliation grow angry and react out of pure self preservation. I know a woman who wore so many labels that her identity was almost completely tied up with a manufactured self. She had lived for many years trying to prove how good she was, and because of this her ego had grown to the size of the church she was the minister of. Her character had become proud, defensive, and controlling, and because of her constant need to keep on projecting this persona, life was exhausting for her, which in turn made her irritable and childishly bad tempered. There was one occasion when she exploded with such rage that it triggered an emotional breakdown, and I am convinced that this *could* have been the place of healing. This could have been the place where she took a major step in re-discovering her own inner gold and beauty, and how loved she was *without her trying to prove anything*. Yet such was the power of her ego (which could not bear the humiliation of the fall) and the collusion of her family (who also could not bear the humiliation) that she simply avoided the gift of humility and got over the experience by blaming outside forces. She even began to use terminology to describe the breakdown that was inaccurate and gave a completely different picture from the one that was true. Sadly, today she seems to be as unliberated as ever.

So the hitting of rock bottom is not an automatic reconnection to our true selves, but it can be. It can potentially be the most precious gift we could imagine, and therefore perhaps the *bottom* of the ladder is the place we ought to stay, or at least visit.

I want to use the next two chapters to explore both those possibilities. How can we *stay* for longer at the bottom of the ladder – the place of the crack that reveals the inner gold? And, if not stay, how can we *visit* that place?

CHAPTER TEN

STAYING WITH THE TREASURE

The spirituality of Alcoholics Anonymous will go down in history as the significant and authentic American contribution to the history of spirituality.

[12] **Richard Rohr.**

One spiritual (though not religious) community that really knows how to *stay with the treasure* is the worldwide fellowship known as Alcoholics Anonymous. AA follows a spiritual therapy course known as the Twelve Step Programme and I had the privilege of belonging to a twelve-step group for about two years. I call it a privilege because I had never before, and have never since, met such beautifully humble, honest, and wise people. They had been to hell and back literally, yet were like shining stars.

I first decided to go along to AA because I was worried about my own potential of becoming an alcoholic. It was in the days following my divorce and I was regularly bringing drink home as a way of coping with the turmoil. Though I later discovered that I was not alcoholic I will never regret being part of the group, and (this might sound crazy) sometimes I am even a little envious of my AA friends who seem to have been taken much further into the experience of their true inner gold than myself.

I remember one meeting where this guy said, 'Hello I'm (name) and I am *delighted* that I am an alcoholic', and he could say that because it was true. He had been in recovery for about thirty years and told me he would not change *anything* about his life, even the destructive hell of his pre-AA alcoholic days. The fact that he had hit rock bottom thirty years before, and had handed over his life to God, had brought him so many blessings. He had not only discovered his own gold, but he had been privileged to witness many others (hundreds) come to the realisation of their own inner gold too. The experiences that being in AA had given him were totally priceless.

When I first sat through an AA meeting I was flabbergasted by the clientele. I should not have made assumptions, but I expected to see a group of what we might call 'down and outs', and largely male at that. It was a revelation to discover that the room was full of men and women from every conceivable background, age and profession, and now they were about to absorb a young middle-class clergyman into their community.

The second thing that I became aware of, as I listened to their stories, was their brutal honesty about their lives. They held nothing back, and allowed their group of trusted friends and co-sufferers into their very deepest and darkest secrets.

I remember wondering whether this was what the phrase in the New Testament 'confess your sins to one another' (James 5:16) really meant; a deep sharing of human flaws and failings in a context of non-judgement and the warm embrace of fellow frail humans.

A word that I noticed being used time and time again was powerlessness, and I soon began to realise that the admission of personal powerlessness was the place from where they began their recovery. The first of the Twelve Steps in the programme is to admit that one is powerless, and that life has become unmanageable. I am told it is the hardest step to take, not simply because it is the first, but because of the will of the ego to do everything in its power to avoid humiliation. Strong people simply don't do that; they don't admit to their deepest faults. They cope, they survive, they control. Yet I was soon to discover that the taking of the first step was the *strongest* thing anyone could do – even for a non-alcoholic. To come to the place where you know you have no power to help yourself is like hitting rock bottom. On the one hand you feel broken and humbled, yet on the other hand you have stopped falling. You can't sink any lower, and (as is so often the case in AA) there is suddenly a tiny glimmer of light, and an inner voice that says 'things can be different now'.

The humility I witnessed as people spoke of what it's like to live with such powerlessness was like nothing I'd ever experienced before. As a priest it was how I so longed for the church to be. I wished the practice of confession (be it public or private) could be so honest and potentially liberating. I truly believe that the place of powerlessness is not just the place from which alcoholics and addicts need to come in order to find light, but is the place where all people need to come, and I am sad that so often organised religion fails to bring people there.

To quote a rather over-used phrase from the New Testament, 'All have sinned and fall short of the glory of God' (Romans 3:23). As I said earlier in this book, not one of us is perfect. Sin affects us all. For some it's the 'more obvious' sins as expressed by the first son in the Parable of the Two Lost Sons (drunkenness, debauchery, and so on), and for others it's the less obvious sins as expressed by the second son (spiritual pride, arrogance, self assuredness). Whatever our sinful tendency is, we all need to spend time on our knees confessing, and admitting how far short of God's glory we are, for that is the place of healing and Grace.

Consider this! St Paul is (apart from Jesus himself) the most important person in the story of Christianity. I know that for some he is not the most popular figure in the story, but without Paul's missions and epistles we would probably not have become a universal religion at all. Yet look at this admission/confession that Paul made in his own writings:

For I know that nothing good dwells in me, that is, in my flesh; for the wishing is present in me, but the doing of the good is not.

For the good that I wish, I do not do; but I practise the very evil that I do not wish. (Romans 7:18-19 *NASB*)

Confession is to be radically honest about who we are and our capability for getting it wrong. It is to allow ourselves to weep and have our hearts broken before God. If we never have our hearts broken, and if we never feel we need to say sorry, then we will consequently never experience the beauty and transformative power of forgiveness. This kind of breaking of heart and radical honesty is the way AA works. In fact the programme would not work without it.

Another thing I discovered among my AA friends was that they did not see the taking of the first step as a thing of the past. They do not say to themselves, 'I took Step One and admitted I was powerless seventeen years ago, and have been sober ever since'. No, they live with the taking of the first step on a *daily* basis. AA people never say they been cured or healed; they say they are 'in recovery'. They do not claim to have once been an alcoholic; they see themselves as alcoholics who will try not to take a drink *today*.

Every time a person speaks within an AA meeting they will begin by saying, 'I am *(name)* and I am an alcoholic'. This is, once more, to remind them and everyone else that they are still coming from the place of powerlessness. So in reality they are standing on the rock at the bottom of the ladder, *and they are not budging* because they know that it is the place of recovery and Grace.

I find it so exciting that a self-help programme for alcoholics and addicts has lead us to exactly the same place that many spiritual paths have also lead us. For example, it is the place that St Francis and his followers call poverty, the Carmelite tradition calls nothingness, the Buddhist tradition calls emptiness, and Jesus called hunger or thirst (Luke 6:21), childlikeness (Matthew 18:1-4), lostness (Matthew 18:12-14) or even sinfulness (Luke 5:31,32).

I believe the Twelve Step movement has authenticated the other spiritualities that were so often seen as only for those who were 'spiritual people'. They are all saying we need to stay empty and therefore open to a higher power. We need to surrender and thus become ready for transformation.

This is also the gift that true humility brings, and I have never met as many truly humble people as my AA friends. As Gerard Hughes says:

'The Humble... are aware of their own fragility, of their own failings and sinfulness, but they are not preoccupied with them. Such preoccupation would be an inverted form of pride, replacing God at the centre of our lives in favour of our rotten selves! Humble people surrender their ego to the goodness and greatness of God,

and in so doing they experience a wonderful sense of freedom; the freedom of which St Paul writes in his second letter to the Corinthians: 'For our sake God made the sinless one into sin, so that in him we might become the goodness of God' (2Cor.5: 21), and again to the Galatians: 'I live now not with my own life but with the life of Christ who lives in me' (Gal.2: 20). The humble catch glimpses of this truth. In losing life, in letting go of their own ego, they discover a much fuller life. Clinging to nothing, they possess all things; letting go of their securities, they discover that God really is their rock, their refuge and their strength. Through humility, they catch a glimpse of the wisdom of the God who put aside his own divinity and became one of us, so that we might find our true identity, which is to be at one with God and with all creation.'

[13] **Gerard Hughes.**

Step Two of Alcoholics Anonymous calls members to not only admit their powerlessness but assert that they have 'come to believe that God can restore their sanity'.

I must point out that AA is not a Christian movement nor is it affiliated to any religion, spiritual tradition or philosophy. It unashamedly uses the term God but qualifies the term by adding 'as you understand him'.

What I find so exciting about this belief in a God who restores our sanity is that it is the one step that seems to happen *without effort*. All of the other steps require effort and action. The first step requires the admission of something that is very difficult to express: personal powerlessness. Step Three requires a decision to hand everything over to God, Step Four requires the taking of a self-conscious and critical look at oneself. Step Two simply states that 'we came to believe…'. It is as if the natural consequence of admitting to powerlessness and ending up on that rock at the bottom is the entry point for God and the power of his presence. This ties in precisely with what I was saying in Chapter Eight, The Treasure and the Clay. Step Two is about the natural discovery of the gold through the cracks we have experienced. We are fallen and broken open only to discover that the presence of God (the inner gold) is there within us.

The two great lessons from AA that help us to stay with the treasure are: 1) Be radically honest about yourself. See yourself exactly as you are underneath all those hats and masks you wear. And, 2) Know that the real you is loved and held and valued by God, a God who you will find down there in the depths and who will be your strength.

Of course it is highly unrealistic to claim that anyone can stay with the treasure eternally. We are all human and we will all at some point start to try and control, climb, change and basically do God's job for him. As I've tried to say before, many of us are actually doing this *most of the time.* So, if we cannot continually stay with it, how can we visit the treasure from time to time?

This is the question I will be asking in the next chapter.

(Note: Of course the next ten steps are also spiritual dynamite, and I strongly recommend that anyone who is serious about the spiritual journey go and dig out some books, or consult the Web on the AA's Twelve Step Programme.)

CHAPTER ELEVEN

VISITING THE TREASURE

There's something else inside us that is precious. A precious pearl. A treasure. The reign of God is inside us. If we would only discover that! The great tragedy of life lies not in how much we suffer but in how much we miss. Human beings are born asleep, live asleep, and die asleep. Maybe we're not born asleep; we're born awake, but as the brain develops, we fall asleep. We have children asleep, raise children asleep, handle big business deals asleep, enter government office asleep, and die asleep. We never wake up. This is what spirituality is about: waking up. We're living in a drunken stupor. It's as though we were hypnotised, drugged! And we don't know what we're missing. How to get out of this? How to wake up? How are we going to know we're asleep?

[14] **Anthony de Mello.**

In the last chapter I talked about the great phenomenon of Alcoholics Anonymous and how it has authenticated some of the teachings of other (perhaps less grounded) spiritual traditions. AA has literally worked wonders with millions of broken men and women and has taken them to the place where they can see their own true worth (inner gold), and this has radically changed their lives. Linking the AA experience with the experience of any of us who go through brokenness and falls, I tried to give some clues as to how we might stay for longer with the experience of seeing the treasure. But, let's be honest here, modern life simply does not make it possible for us to stay in that place for long. We have huge demands on us; families to look after; jobs to do; churches to run; expectations to meet. Very quickly we can be placed back on the treadmill again.

Yet there is hope. There is hope in the form of an ancient spiritual practise that will allow us to visit our inner treasure. I am speaking of the worldwide and multi-religious practise of meditation. No matter how important (or busy) a role we have in life, mediation can help keep us close to who we truly are.

Of course meditation is simple but not easy. When we meditate we seek to become alert and aware in a way that normal (mind-dominating) life does not encourage. Meditation is not about going off into a dream state or falling asleep. In fact it's the exact opposite – it's about waking up, waking up from a dream (the dream that is the treadmill of life).

We usually live our lives in the future, wishing for this or that to be different, or in the past, regretting, resenting, and even wishing we were back there. Neither the future nor the past is real. They exist only in our minds as mental projections. Of course the past happened and the future will happen, but we are not in either place NOW. Today we are *here*. Meditation is about helping us to re-connect with the present moment and live in the NOW, and now is where the gold of our true self exists.

Many people who meditate regularly begin to notice that they start living more and more in the present moment, and thus sense a reconnection of mind and body. It is, however, important to realise that meditation is not about a 'goal' to achieve. If anything, meditation helps us to see that the goal is already here. It's just like the story The Egg of Gold, where the searcher for hidden treasure, after a long and fruitless journey, finally gives up, and only then realises that the treasure is actually back at home where he began. Inside every one of us is a treasure more precious than any chest of gold. It is the *same treasure* that we find through the cracks after our falls. Meditation helps us to begin to see it again. It pulls back the layers that we have allowed to suffocate our true Selves.

But how do we do it? How do we meditate? How do we quieten the ceaseless flow of thoughts and confusions that buzz incessantly round our minds, and keep us either in the future or the past?

One tradition that can be found in Christianity, Buddhism, Hinduism and many other places is the use of the *mantra*. A mantra is a single word or short phrase that is repeated over and over again during a period of meditation. It keeps the mind (the little-me) occupied and in a sense stops the inner chatter, helping us to gradually re-awaken the experience of being alive and alert NOW. It can be said verbally but it is usually said inwardly. The important thing is to keep saying the mantra calmly and without any sense of hurry.

What should one use as a mantra? Well it could literally be any word or phrase you choose, even one from a different language to your own. In fact, for me using my own language is likely to conjure up associations or spark off my over active imagination, so I find it better to use one from a different language. Some Christians have found great profit using the Aramaic word 'maranatha' which means 'come lord'. I myself (after beginning a new language course) use a Swahili word, 'Nina-amka', which means 'I awaken'. It really does not matter what the word or phrase is. The important thing is to stick to it. Some Zen practitioners simply count from 'One' to 'Ten' over and over again as their 'mantra'.

The mantra is not magic. It's simply meant to help concentration, so our thoughts begin to slow down and eventually stand still. As I said, meditation is simple but not easy. Saying the mantra (especially when one first starts) takes a great deal of determination. If you get bored or distracted you must carry on, always re-focussing on the saying of the mantra if your mind wanders, and wander it will! Don't worry about wandering thoughts, and don't worry if it seems like you are getting no-where. Let me repeat, meditation is not a race, and it's not about getting anywhere, *but being here*. Just keep gently guiding yourself back to the mantra. It will do its own work.

So how do we begin to meditate? Sit comfortably, either in a chair with your back straight and feet firmly on the floor, or on a cushion, with back straight and legs crossed. It's important to be relaxed and comfortable, but alert and attentive. You might like to close your eyes so as to focus inwardly. However I personally find this increases my imaginative thoughts, so I tend to allow my eyes to remain just slightly open so I can half-focus on the ground in front of me. Allow you hands to rest where it feels natural, perhaps with palms open and upward. Begin to take some deep breaths and start to allow yourself to relax. After breathing deeply for a while you can begin to say the mantra. If it has two syllables, like the word 'abba' say 'a' on the in-breath and 'baa' on the out-breath. Four syllable words like Nina-amka also fit to this rhythm, 'nina' on the in-breath and 'amka' on the out-breath. The important thing is to gently allow yourself to say the mantra in some sort of rhythmic way, like a pulse.

When it begins to feel natural you may try watching/following your breath as it enters and leaves your body (still saying the mantra of course). This observation of your breathing can help to develop a real awareness of your body, and of all the sensations and movements of it. You may even begin to feel your actual heart beat, and be aware of the blood flowing around your body as the heart pumps away.

Focus on the saying of the mantra. Don't look for results, fruit will come anyway. Just allow the mantra to do its own work in your life.

CHAPTER TWELVE

THE BREAKING OF JESUS

[So] *why the death of Christ? The death of Christ was necessary for this reason – if Jesus in his love had stopped short of the Cross, it would have meant that there was somewhere beyond which the love of God could not go, and there was something beyond which God could not forgive. On the Cross God says to us in Jesus Christ: 'Nothing – absolutely nothing that you can do – can stop me loving you.'*

[15] **William Barclay.**

It would be impossible, especially as a priest, to write a book about brokenness and vulnerability without concluding with a chapter on the brokenness of Jesus himself. Surely the torture of crucifixion was one of the most horrific types of breaking any human could have been asked to endure.

Am I being perverse in asking the question, 'Did any beams of light shine through the cracks and wounds in Jesus' broken body?' I believe such light does shine from the Cross. I believe there is the most profound gift of pure gold to be found at this place of destruction and pain.

The theological language for the subject of this question is 'The Atonement'; how did Christ's death on the Cross create an

AT-ONE-MENT between God and humankind?

The trouble is that much of what the church has traditionally taught about the atonement is, to be frank, more like chunks of coal than glittering gold. I don't mean to be unfair, but I have heard so much *bad news* spoken about the Cross and salvation that I have sometimes almost given up hope of hearing about the *good news*.

Therefore I want to conclude with this humble offering of my own. But rather than add to the huge amount of academic and intellectual theories of the atonement I simply want to offer one more piece of story magic.

I recently wrote an alternative story to use with the trick that I mentioned in Chapter Two, The Gypsy Thread. If you remember, it involved a piece of yarn which is unwound and burned in various places, only to be rolled up and restored again.

THE PASCHAL THREAD

Once, when the world was a darkened place, and people couldn't seem to see God's face, a light was sent *(strike match and light candle)* and from that moment hope was stirred.

Time passed, and the light grew and gradually those who'd felt so alienated from God began to feel themselves being re-connected. It was as if a great thread had been unwound linking them to heaven, making them feel held in a way they had never felt held before. Even the ones who had been living lives so far from God's ways felt renewed, valued, loved, and blessed. Grace was flowing freely and broken ones were being healed. *(The thread is unwound and stretched out over the candle flame)*

BUT all was not well for there were also those who felt threatened by this new outpouring of Grace. And, though the same gift was available to them, they felt they could do better by trusting in their own goodness, cleverness and religious piety.

And soon they started to fear this light, because he seemed to be taking their place as the bridge between heaven and earth, and so they sought to extinguish it.

They struck out in different ways, testing *(snap the thread over the flame)*, accusing *(snap),* scheming *(snap),* and finally they destroyed him altogether *(blow out the candle)*. And it seemed at that point that the light had gone out for good.

For three days the world sat in darkness. *(Wind up all the broken pieces and pause leaving a dramatic silence)*

But then, out of the silence some strange force began to stir, and suddenly the light that had been extinguished burst back into a new flame. *(Light candle again)*

And the light came back into the world, back into the very world that had killed him. And what's more, he came back, not with any sense of judgement or anger at those who'd abused him so badly, but with a gift. A gift offered to all people, a gift that said, 'YOU can do nothing to destroy God's love for you, for nothing is more powerful than love, it will always find a way of bursting back into life, and know this, that though you *will* make mistakes and from time to time fall down, the thread of life that exists between you and I can never *and will never* be broken.' *(Stretch out the restored thread)*

As Barclay said: '*On the Cross God says to us in Jesus Christ: 'Nothing – absolutely nothing that you can do – can stop me loving you.'*

Amen.

A FINAL EXERCISE:

Take out the 'picture of God' that I suggested you draw in the first exercise of this book.

Would you draw a different picture now?

Has your image of God changed at all?

What would you like to say to this God?

More importantly, what do you think he would like to say to YOU?

CONCLUSION

Please allow me to leave you with one more trick. You will need to have a calculator handy to accomplish this effect… it's worth it, trust me!

Take the number of the *day* of the month, on which you were born,
And multiply it by 4,
Now add 13,
And multiply by 25,
Now subtract 200,
Add the number of the month on which you were born,
And multiply the total by 2,
Now subtract 40, multiply by 50, and add the last two digits of the year in which you were born,
Finally subtract 10,500.

Congratulations! You should now be looking at a very important date in history *(see note below)*. A date on which a very special person, made in God's image and likeness was born… *You*.

Now finally let me remind you of something from the very beginning of this book, and again, *it's about you:*

You are unique.
You are beautiful.
You are made in God's image.
There is no-one like you.
You are special.
You are once only.
You are never to be repeated.

You are incredible.

(Note: For readers in the US the date will be in UK order i.e. day/month/year)

APPENDIX 1

The following piece is the result of an exercise I set for all the local clergy where I work, after being asked to lead a day on 'Priesthood?' I must say my colleagues were not over eager to carry out my exercise, and I can't say I blame them. It must have sounded strange, for I asked them to try to write a letter to themselves about their ministries *as if it were God writing.*

On the day itself most of us had completed the exercise and the time had come to share the letters. What I observed blew my mind for I began to hear about a completely different God than the one we usually talked about in our clergy Bible studies. It was as if writing these letters had opened us up to another dimension of God.

One priest was visibly surprised by her own words and when she'd finished reading her letter she held it close to her heart and said, 'Oh thank you God'.

Now of course I am not claiming that the letters *were* literally from God, but I do think that writing them had put us all (at least partly) in touch with a deeper, wiser part of our own psyches, the 'Divine Me'?

What follows is a short extract of my own letter from that day:

A LETTER FROM 'ME' TO 'ME'

"Mark, it seems from what you just wrote that things are beginning to change for you. That's good! Your words are sounding less negative and you seem to be coming to a place where your inner core is generally happy, and less defensive than in the past. You are learning that you are not in control and all your past attempts to

be in control have only ended up in misery. You are not in control but I am. I am your security.

You still cling, and possess, and look for approval and love in areas that can never give it. You are still addictive and sometimes seek to fill your emptiness with things that are only temporary pleasures. But your journey towards who you really are, or should I say your learning to let go of the false self, is gradually happening."

"Mark, stop it. Turn off that music. Stop trying to be clever and listen NOW. Even now you are distracting yourself.

Mark, how many times do I have to tell you? You try too hard. Even now, most of this is still you trying so hard to find the right words and right thoughts; trying to cleverly articulate your description of priesthood. But you don't need to. It's really very simple and you know it. You – the Church – invented priesthood anyway, and it sometimes works and sometimes doesn't. It can therefore be a good thing or a bad thing. But whatever, you know what it means to you and you know why you are a priest.

You heard the message that you call the Gospel and are gradually allowing it to take hold of your life. You want to share it with others, and perhaps more importantly you see it as your calling to somehow be a sign of this Gospel to others. That's your understanding of priesthood, and that's good. But you also know what stops much of this from happening.

Try to stop trying so hard. Then you might stay for longer in the periods of Grace. Stop analysing and debating with yourself. Stop putting yourself on a guilt trip. Listen to yourself when you

tell others it's all about letting go. Learn to let go yourself, and be silent and listen. Listen to where and how you are being called. For every moment of every day you are being called to something. Sometimes you hear this call and respond, but often you take the easier option and do what's in your diary, or what the ones you seek approval from ask of you.

You are there to walk with others who have responded to this Gospel. But don't allow your false humility to let you imagine you are just walking alongside them. No, there are times when you have the privilege of leading the way too. Don't be shy of this. I communicate with you not for your self alone but for you also to communicate it to others.

Of course people need leadership. Don't you? Where do you go for your spiritual direction? You know where. Well, the rest also need this direction. Do not limit me by imagining I cannot use you in this regard."

APPENDIX 2

AN EPISTLE OF MYSELF

This was written by Patrick Duff, a rock musician from Bristol and participant of the retreat 'The Gospel of Falling Down'. He (and all of us) were stunned and amazed by what came out in this 'epistle'.

"I am here God and I want you to talk to me. I want to ask you why I so often feel afraid of my life and of other people, especially after I have played my songs."

"The truth lies in you calling them 'my songs'. Your songs belong to the universe. They used you as a channel to come through and they reflect the life force and its urge to manifest, using you and everything in you to give expression to itself. When your songs fall under the glance of other egos then you are offended – you fear their eyes are judging you harshly and that they are tearing you apart in the same way you yourself would do. In fact people are afraid and overjoyed and bored and inspired and changed by your songs. There are as many reactions as there are people. In searching for the reaction you want in order to rid yourself of your own fears you suspect the harshness of others because of your own harshness. In fact I have sent you many, many, many people to compliment you in many ways and their number is growing. Why is it you can't accept this? Is it because of your attempts to hide from yourself your own misgivings? These misgivings have their use. They drive you onwards and you must travel great distances now so everything

must be used. The fear and the paranoia are essentially me in another form urging you onwards, keeping you on your toes. The pain that drove you inside to search for me is the same pain that will bring me out into the world through you. Through your songs and your performances, your words and the example of your life, which is the brightest of the most distant stars, I have come to you. I have reached out for you and you have fallen into my arms."

"Will my music be successful? How much longer will it be until I can release my album? I am afraid someone else is going to do my thing better."

"Your life is your life – it has its momentum that cannot be sped up or slowed down by an act of will. Darker forces are at play. You can only be ready when you are ready and the world can only be ready when you are ready. Each day try to push your dream a little forward. Talk to me and do not be afraid to ask for anything you want. In your case all desires will be granted – so desire in small ways and feel your way through the darkness by throwing out small desires, small desires do not limit the scope of your potential by falling into the limited imagination of your ego. I am building you a life with deep roots and firm foundations. If you are out of time then time will change for you. So be it. The structure must firstly penetrate the fire and the earth's centre, the oceans and death. The fish that swim in the deepest caverns must be pulled up and manifest roasted on the fires of the centre of the earth and absorbed in darkness before they can be sent into the light. The light must shine with the fire of the centre of the earth

and be a bridge to the light of the most distant star, the lion and the pyramid. The most distant star that you alone must contact and manifest. Remember the music in the Sacre Coeur and the glimpse you had of its communication with the heart. Something most beautiful is coming. The time is moving and the time is now. Something has moved over you and you are aware of it. Of course you are afraid because this feeling has come before and still nothing is manifest. But think of the facts and the friends you are making.

Once there was a child who lived in the land of the yellow sunset, all day long that child waited for the sunset and every day it came. The child bathed in its yellow light, danced, and sang music and needed no other, for his parents were dead and his sisters had gone to the city to find work. The child fed on the wild locusts and honey of the land. One day the child's sunset did not come for the sun went down and did not return. The child waited and waited, for always the sun had returned each beautiful morning to greet the child and then he watched the chariots pull it across the sky to the yellow sunset, for it was the dying of the sun the child loved. But sunrise was no more. For years the child waited in the darkness. He groped his way through the blackness. He came to a city and found work scrubbing the pavements outside a businessman's house. But he kept in his heart the memory of the dying sun and his hope it would be reborn to die once again. One day the child met an old man. The old man was carrying the sun in his mouth. But the boy could not see the man was doing this. He just saw something in the old man's eyes. And when he played music something awoke in the boy's heart. Slowly the boy began to learn the music

day by day; it was difficult because of the hardship of the boy's life, but he learnt. He had nothing else to distract him. And people began to hear him play. As time went on the boy learnt more and more and grew into a man. He thought of the music when he was scrubbing the floors and at night he played to the people on the street who began to love him. Then the rich people began travelling to see him and they were amazed too. The boy went to the old man who was gone one day. He had left him a note, which was a picture of the yellow sunset. The boy put the picture on his wall and remembered. He played the music until the world began to fall in love with him. Then one day the sun rose again. The boy's heart was filled with joy. It was the sunrise he loved now. It was the rising of the first morning once again. The people of the city did not know that it had been the boy who had raised up the sun by his music, but the boy didn't mind for he knew. He knew he had lit up the world again. And the old man spoke to him. He told the boy that one day he would have to swallow the sun again and plunge the city into darkness, so all would be desolate. Why? the boy asked. The old man told him this:

Your ways are not my ways. I am the voice of the stars and of distant galaxies. Nothing can ever last forever. So I need some people to carry the light in them so that they can pass it on to others. The earth must see that until the sun is appreciated chosen ones will carry it in their mouths to pass on through the times of most darkness. And it is the chosen few who must swallow the sun and plunge everyone else into darkness until they find another child to light once again. One day the world will neither live nor die nor swallow the sun. Until that day only

music can speak for me.

You are blessed, Patrick, far, far beyond anything you understand. You are the child and the old man simultaneously and over and over again throughout time. Go back into my world again without fear and accept the vast riches I will give you without guilt or hesitation. Pass them on and swallow the sun. Again and again and again."

APPENDIX 3

21st-CENTURY CANA

AN IMAGINATIVE RE-TELLING OF JESUS' FIRST MIRACLE BY A MAGICIAN/PRIEST

The Bible is an enchanting book, and if we allow ourselves to enter into the mystery, wonder and spellbindingly magical world of scripture by putting our over-rational minds to one side for a while, then I believe it can come alive to us like never before. I must add that both theological conservatives and theological liberals are as capable as each other at being fixated with rational arguments over scripture. Let's remember that primarily it is *story* – and it is story filled with mythology, poetry, fable and fact. In our lust for the facts let's not miss the mystery.

This is my re-telling of Jesus' miracle of turning water into wine. I hope it encourages you to pick up that old black leather-bound book, blow off the dust and immerse yourselves in a world of life-changing, spine-tingling magic.

Have any of you ever had one of those experiences that are so earth shattering and spine-tingling that you're just left standing there in silence and wide-eyed wonder? I have.

It was a few years ago now, and I happened to be conducting a wedding ceremony for a Middle Eastern man and an Asian woman. They were a beautiful couple; they looked like a prince and princess straight out of the Arabian Nights.

I was kindly invited to the reception, which was a held in the grounds of a huge country manor. They had two great marquees and an enormous bouncy castle in the style of the pink castle from Disney world for the kids. There was exotic traditional entertainment in the form of Arabian dancers and wonderful Eastern music. There even a Fakir, a strolling magician with a turban, snake basket and a magic flute. He seemed to be able to work real magic, with all his flashes of light and coloured smoke. It was awesome!

And then there were the guests: I tell you I've never seen so many people at a wedding reception, and from every place on earth it seemed. To be honest I thought I was in heaven.

Now the couple clearly came from very important families. You could tell that by the sheer scale of the reception; the food, the wine, the guests, the setting...

I remember being introduced to both sets of parents. They were so kind about the wedding ceremony that I performed, and they showed me genuinely warm Eastern hospitality. But it was the bride's father who stood out. My God, what an impressive guy! There was something about him. I don't know what it was. All I can say is that he was almost regal, or was it chivalrous. He looked and carried himself like I imagine the great Sala-ha-din to have.

Anyway time went on, and more guests arrived. And then something odd happened. For a moment it all went quiet. It was as if time had momentarily stopped. People stood almost frozen, facing towards one of the marquee entrances. I couldn't make out what (or who) it was they were gazing at.

Then, just as suddenly, the spell was broken and everything was back to normal again; the chatter, the laughter, the celebration, the dancing.

It was like those occasions when you look at your watch and the second hand seems to have got stuck. Has that ever happened to you? It seems to take longer than a second to move, and then it does. Well imagine that, only the pause lasts for about ten seconds.

A few more hours passed, the temperature was rising, a couple of guests were getting a little drunk, and the music and dancers were still working their visual and audible magic. And even though there were a few half-cut guests around there was no sense of nastiness or negativity, just a great joyful and deeply loving atmosphere.

And then I saw his face, the bride's father. Now for a man like him to be looking like that something must have been wrong. He looked, how can I put it, as if the weight of the world had fallen upon his shoulders.

As the priest I thought I'd better go over and see what the problem was but I was more than a little nervous. He wouldn't talk.

I learned later that he couldn't face me out of embarrassment. Embarrassment! What had happened to make the guy so embarrassed?

Well I'll tell you. I managed, you see, to pick up from one of the waiters that a couple of hours before, a new guest had arrived with his mother, but he'd also brought a whole group of his friends with him, and it was no small number. Now, this in itself was no problem at all. The bride's father would have normally been delighted to welcome a hundred more unannounced guests. However, today was different. There had been a miscalculation on the part of the wedding co-ordinator. He had accidentally not ordered enough wine; they were approximately twenty cases short. (You have to understand this reception was not a one-day affair.)

Without the extra guests, the wine would have lasted a couple more hours (enough time for someone to go and collect the extra cases) but now that there were about forty or fifty more thirsts to quench they would be lucky to last fifteen minutes.

The bride's father was looking sick with worry because he was about to lose face in front of the most important people in his world. He was really very upset. There was only one person tenser in the whole place, and that was the poor co-ordinator. Thankfully the bride and groom and most of the other close family members had not yet had the news broken to them, so they remained in blissful ignorance, but how much longer before their day would also be ruined?

Can you remember I mentioned the feeling of time standing still? Well it was about now that another such experience happened. It was similar yet different. I noticed some movement over near the water fountains. Just to explain, as it was an Eastern wedding it was customary for all the guests to wash and purify their hands before sitting down to the meal, a lovely custom that's both practical and symbolic. The co-ordinator had managed to rig up a very elegant looking fountain with six shoots of water. It looked spellbinding, especially considering all the coloured spotlights inside the marquee. It was almost like a mini Jean Michel Jarre open-air concert where he uses great water fountains and coloured light to shoot out in time to the music.

So, there was this movement going on over there near the fountain, and that's when the second strange experience occurred. This time is was not like a great pause in time, but a kind of tremor, a non-physical rush that seemed to bounce out from the fountain point like ripples in a pond. It only lasted a few moments, but I could feel a sensation running through me; a pulse; a heartbeat; wave of energy; that's all I can describe. Strange isn't it. I don't know what it was but something happened.

I'm coming to the end of this little story, and I've described two of the things that happened that day, each of which were kind of unsettling to say the least, but the third experience was to have an impact like nothing else I can remember.

You see, an hour or so after the feeling of those waves of energy hitting me, I suddenly realised that it was now way past the fifteen minutes that I'd been told the wine would last for. I suddenly grew a little inquisitive and went over to find the bride's father again. And there I saw him beaming, holding a glass in his hand; with all those cares and worries now completely removed from his face. In fact he looked better than he had all day.

I saw the co-ordinator too, and likewise he looked fantastic. What on earth had happened? Well I can't answer that. I guess somehow they managed to get a super quick delivery, or even rustled up something from the exclusive manor house wine cellar. Thinking about it, it must have been the latter because everyone was saying how the wine had actually got better in quality as the night went on, and it was pretty wonderful to start with.

Anyway I turned round, happy and relieved that the party was not going to end in anyone's embarrassment or shame, and found myself looking into what can only be described as the most remarkable, enchanting, love-filled, and all together gracious face I've ever seen in my entire life. I don't know who he was, or were he was from, or even why he was there. After all, he didn't seem to be elegantly dressed like the rest of the guests. But he stopped me in my tracks, and without even saying a word to him or hearing any words from him, I KNEW, I JUST KNEW THAT HE WAS THE REASON WHY IT HAD ALL WORKED OUT AS IT DID.

That's when I felt myself standing in silence and wide-eyed wonder. He was so human, yet he wasn't. He was strangely authoritative, yet there was no sense of judgement or threat in his eyes. He was special, yet he made me feel special.

I can't remember anything much after that. All I know is that I went home changed. I knew that I'd met someone who'd taught me more about myself than I ever knew before. He taught me that I could change water into wine; lead into gold, the ordinary into the extraordinary, and so can you!

APPENDIX 4

I have included the following because it was how I decided to close the Gospel of Falling Down Retreat. I wrote this Eucharistic Prayer because I was so unsatisfied with the 'official' ones. Admittedly some of them are so much better than the last lot (Alternative Service Book of 1980), but (in my opinion) they still fail to paint an adequate picture of God's unconditional love and, if the Eucharist is about anything, surely it's about gratefully immersing ourselves in precisely that love. If you have the opportunity please do feel free to use these following prayers.

A LITURGY OF UNCONDITIONAL LOVE BY MARK TOWNSEND

Welcome:

The Creator is here
His Image is within us

The Saviour is here
His Grace is upon us

The Spirit is here
His Power is among us

Made in His Image
Saved by His Grace

Filled with His Power
We enter Sacred Space

Song:

Confession:

(Silence for personal reflection)

Words of God's forgiveness:

May the God, whose love excludes no one,
Whose Grace is all embracing,
Hold, heal and forgive us.
In the name of Christ.
AMEN

(Optional) Kyrie or Gloria:

Reading (s):

Word (talk / drama / meditation / story etc.):

Prayers:

Song (gifts brought to altar):

Prayer over gifts:
Bread of creation,

Fruit of the vineyards.

Gifts of the earth,
Made by our hands.

Lord take them, bless them, and return them to us
That we may be transformed.

Prayer of thanksgiving:

God our Creator, we give you thanks,
for your most precious gift of Christ Our Lord.
He is the Word made flesh,
both human and divine,
holding together heaven and earth
in one eternal relationship.

He opened his arms to embrace us all –
yet we chose to pierce his precious hands,
and nail him naked to a cross of wood.

There he remained in agony and pain
until his final breath;
held fast not by nails,
or by men,
but by LOVE –
unconditional love for all.

(Pause)

This love cannot be extinguished.
This love has conquered death,
for after three days You *raised him up*
and exalted him to your right hand.

And so with saints and sages,
angels and apostles,
and with the whole cosmic family of Christ,
we praise our heavenly Lord by saying
(singing)...

Holy, holy, holy Lord,
God of power and might,
Heaven and earth are full of your glory.
Hosanna in the highest.

Loving Father inspire our imaginations
and take us back to that awesome place where,
gathered round a table with his friends,
Jesus took bread,
blessed it,
then tore it apart and gave it to them saying,
'Take this, and eat it, for this is my body, given for you.
Do this, and remember – me.'

Then he took hold of the cup, blessed it,
and gave it to them saying,
'Take this and drink deeply,
for this is the blood of the new relationship with God.

Do this, and remember – me.'

How great is the mystery of faith!

Christ has died,
Christ is risen,
Christ will come again.

Lord Jesus Christ,
you are with us and among us.
As we now join your first friends
in that upstairs room,
so breathe upon us, and upon these gifts,
that they may be heaven's nourishment to us,
comforting,
renewing,
upholding and healing,
and we may be your Body,
loving and holding your world.
Amen.

(Silence)

We raise our hearts to heaven and pray:

Abba, Father,
May your name be ever hallowed.
May your kingdom come among us.
May your will be done in all things.

Give us all our daily needs.
Forgive us all our daily sins.
Help us to be forgiving.
Hold us tight in times of trial.
Keep us from falling from your path.
Spare us from evil,
And all that seeks to destroy us,
That we may reach our full potential in Christ.
For it is your reign,
Your power,
Your glory,
Your gift of love,
For now and all eternity.
AMEN.

Look, the bread of life has been broken –
spilling out God's love for the world.

(Optional) *Agnus Dei* sung or played:

So come now to Christ's Table,
where all are welcomed and none are refused,
and receive his gifts of Grace given for you.

Music (or meditative video) played during communion:

Prayer for after communion:

Abba, Father,

we give you thanks for your gift of unconditional love,
the sacrificial giving of yourself,
symbolised by broken bread and blood red wine.
Our hearts have been inspired.
Our faith has been renewed.
Now send us out in the Spirit's power,
to share your love with all.
AMEN.

Song:

Blessing:
Now, as we go on our way,
May the whole company of heaven pray for us,
May the angels watch over and care for us,
And may God the Trinity bless us,
And all Creation,
This day and for ever.
AMEN.

NOTES

1. *You Are The Light*, O Books 2003.
2. *Enfolded in Love – Daily Readings with Julian of Norwich*, published by Darton Longman and Todd 1980.
3. *Choice, Desire and the Will of God*, published by SPCK 2003.
4. *Radical Grace, Daily Meditations*, published by St Anthony Messenger Press 1995
5. *On Being Liked*, published by Darton Longman and Todd 2003.
6. *You Are The Light*? O Books 2003.
7. *More about Mark*, published by SPCK 2001.
8. *Radical Grace, Daily Meditations*, published by St Anthony Messenger Press 1995.
9. *You Are The Light*, O Books 2003.
10. *Walking on Water*, published by Columba Press 1998.
11. *Sacred Journey: Spiritual Wisdom for Times of Transition*, published by Lion Hudson plc 2000.
12. *Radical Grace*, published by St. Anthony Messenger Press 1995.
13. *God In All Things*, published by Hodder and Stoughton 2003.
14. *Walking on Water*, published by Columba Press 1998.
15. *Crucified and Crowned*, published by Arthur James Ltd 1960.

SOME RECENT O BOOKS

An Introduction to Radical Theology

The death and resurrection of God

Trevor Greenfield

This is a clearly written and scholarly introduction to radical theology that, at the same time, provides a contextualised and much needed survey of the movement. At times and in turns Greenfield is passionate, ironical, polemical and acerbic. An underlying wit surfaces in images that punctuate the text. This work is a significant and valuable addition to the literature available not only on theological writing but also cultural change. Journal of Beliefs and Values

1905047606 208pp £12.99 $29.95

Censored Messiah

The truth about Jesus Christ

Peter Cresswell

This revolutionary theory about the life of Jesus and the origins of Christianity describes his role in the Nazorean movement, linked to the Essenes and other contemporary groups opposed to Roman rule-one that reflected the tensions between active revolt and the expectation for divine deliverance. The gospels do provide narrative and an explanation for something that really happened, but were censored and edited by later followers after the destruction of Jerusalem to disguise Jesus' Jewish roots an protect sources.

190381667X 248pp £9.99 $14.95

Everything is a Blessing

Make your life a little easier, less stressful and more meaningful

David Vennells

Looks to the spiritual traditions of East and West, the path of "others" rather than the path of "self". Lasting personal growth is not achieved by solving problems for our own benefit, but following a more broadminded, spiritual and longer-term approach.

1905047223 160pp £11.99 $19.95

God Calling

A Devotional Diary

A. J. Russell

46th printing

Perhaps the best-selling devotional book of all time, over 6 million copies sold.

1905047428 280pp 135/95mm £7.99 cl.

US rights sold

How to Meet Yourself

...and find true happiness

Dennis Waite

A comprehensive survey of the psychological and philosophical dynamics of the human condition, offering an everlasting solution to discovering true happiness in the moment. I highly recommend it. Dennis Waite is one of the foremost contemporary writers on Advaita Vedanta in the West. Paula Marvelly, author of The Teachers of One.

1846940419 260pp £11.99 $24.95

I Still Haven't Found What I'm Looking For

Paul Walker

Traditional understandings of Christianity may not be credible perhaps they can still speak to us in a different way. Perhaps they point to something which we can still sense. Something we need in our lives. Something not just to make us decent, or responsible, but happy and fulfilled. Paul Walker, former Times preacher of the year, does not give answers, but rejoices in the search.

1905047762 144pp £9.99 $16.95

One Self

Life as a means of transformation

Philip Jacobs

This is a compelling and life enhancing book for anyone having to face a long term illness, but also so wise that it can help any of us to understand our path in life even if we are not so severely challenged.

Peter Fenwick, Scientific and Medical Network

1905047673 160pp £9.99 $19.95

The Book of One

The spiritual path of Advaita

Dennis Waite

3rd printing

A masterful and profoundly insightful survey of the Advaita teaching and the contemporary scene.

Alan Jacobs, Chair, Ramana Maharshi Foundation UK.

1903816416 288pp £9.99 $17.95

The Creative Christian

God and us; Partners in Creation

Adrian B. Smith

Enlivening and stimulating, the author presents a new approach to Jesus and the Kingdom he spoke of, in the context of the evolution of our Universe. He reveals its meaning for us of the 21st century. Hans Schrenk, Lecturer in Holy Scripture and Biblical Languages, Middlesex University.

1905047754 160pp £11.99 $24.95

The Gay Disciple

Jesus' friend tells it his own way

John Henson

John offers the reflective reader a perspective on incidents and characters which at the very least make one think and which often help sharpen ones perception of what was, or might have been, going on. He manages to combine the strengths of the Sunday papers columnist approach with the radical evangelical message delivery of one who invites you to think! Meic Phillips ONE co-ordinator

184694001X 128pp £9.99 $19.95

The Jain Path: Ancient Wisdom for the West

Aidan Rankin

The best introduction to Jainism available. It is at once very topical, clear and engaging. David Frawley (Pandit Vamdeva Shastri), Director of the American Institute of Vedic Studies

1905047215 240pp £11.99 $22.95

The Laughing Jesus

Religious lies and Gnostic wisdom

Timothy Freke and Peter Gandy

The Laughing Jesus is a manifesto for Gnostic mysticism. Freke and Gandy's exposition of Gnostic enlightenment is lucid and accessible; their critique of Literalist religion is damningly severe. Robert M. Price, Professor of scriptural studies, editor of The Journal of Higher Criticism

1905047819 272pp £9.99

The Supreme Self

The way to enlightenment

S. Abhayananda

A wonderful synopsis of mystical religions and their numinous goals. Swami Abhayananda is a true teacher. Jack Haas, author of The Way of Wonder

1905047452 224pp £10.99 $19.95

The Trouble With God

Building the republic of heaven

David Boulton

Revised edition

A wonderful repository of religious understanding and a liberal theologian's delight. Modern Believing

1905047061 272pp £11.99 $24.95

The Wisdom of Vedanta

An introduction to the philosophy of non-dualism

S. Abhayananda

Tomorrow's Christian

A new framework for Christian living

Adrian B. Smith

This is a vision of a radically new kind of Christianity. While many of the ideas here have been accepted by radical Christians and liberal theologians for some time, this presents them as an accessible, coherent package: a faith you can imagine living out with integrity in the real world. And even if you already see yourself as a "progressive Christian" or whatever label you choose to adopt, you'll find ideas in both books that challenge and surprise you. Highly recommended. Movement

1903816971 176pp £9.99 $15.95

Tomorrow's Faith

A new framework of Christian belief

Adrian B. Smith

2nd printing

This is the most significant book for Christian thinking so far this millennium. If this does not become a standard textbook for theological and ministerial education, then shame on the institutions! Revd Dr Meic Phillips, Presbyterian

1905047177 128pp £9.99 $19.95